From his earliest childhood, Walter Scott grew to love the legends and stories of Scotland's Border country. When he was only three he went to stay with his grandparents at the farm they rented at Sandyknowe, between Melrose and Kelso. He learnt many stories of Border history from his grandmother, and read many more for himself, while Smailholm Tower, rising above the farm on its 680-feet rock escarpment, provided him with a near-perfect example of the kind of Border keep occupied by the bold knights and barons of medieval times.

Just to climb the steep and rocky path to the tower on its high crag was spur enough for the boy's imagination. He would sit and watch the breeze ruffle the surface of Eden Water below the tower, or look beyond the Dryburgh Abbey and the Eildon Hills to the west, Hume Castle to the east and the Cheviots to the south, in his mind peopling the whole landscape with stirring events from the past.

Sandyknowe Farm and Smailholm Tower were the property of Hugh Scott of Harden, and Walter Scott was staying at Scott of Harden's Home, Mertoun House, in 1799 when he heard that Smailholm was to be demolished. Scott pleaded for it to be spared, and Scott of Harden agreed – provided Walter write a ballad about it. Thus the *Eve of Saint John* came to be written. It was among Scott's earliest works, and was published in Kelso in 1800, two years before *The Minstrelsy of the Scottish Border*. The ballad was a romance of guilty love, murder and revenge, overlaid with the supernatural.

Janice Anderson and Edmund Swinglehurst

Scottish Walks and Legends

The Lowlands and East Scotland

A MAYFLOWER BOOK

GRANADA

London Toronto Sydney New York

Published by Granada Publishing Limited in 1982

ISBN 0 583 13444 0

A Granada Paperback Original
Copyright © Janice Anderson and Edmund Swinglehurst 1982

Granada Publishing Limited
Frogmore, St Albans, Herts AL2 2NF
and
36 Golden Square, London W1R 4AH
866 United Nations Plaza, New York, NY 10017, USA
117 York Street, Sydney, NSW 2000, Australia
100 Skyway Avenue, Rexdale, Ontario, M9W 3A6, Canada
61 Beach Road, Auckland, New Zealand

Printed and bound in Great Britain
by Cox and Wyman Ltd, Reading
Set in Plantin

Granada ®
Granada Publishing ®

CONTENTS

ACKNOWLEDGEMENTS

Quotations from the ballads of *Kinmont Willie* and *Thomas the Rhymer* are from the version published in *The New Oxford Book of Ballads*, James Kinsley (ed.), London 1969.

Photographs on pages 31, 70, 76, 93, 99, 125, 141, 179 are supplied by the British Tourist Authority; all the other photographs by Edmund Swinglehurst.

INTRODUCTION

Stories of monsters, demons, witches and the faery people are common throughout Scotland, as are tales of feuds and vendettas in families and between clans. Like most legendary or semi-legendary events whose details have been passed down through generations, they represent a subconscious well of feeling about the places where people live.

With Scottish legends, a discernible difference in the way in which the stories are recounted may be found between the two broad cultural areas which may be divided roughly by a line drawn from Nairn in the north-east on the Moray Firth, to Glasgow and the Firth of Clyde in the south-west.

To the north and west of this rough frontier lies Celtic Scotland where the Gaelic language may still be heard; to the south and east is a more polyglot area shared by the remnants of Picts and Caledonians, of Britons from Northumbria, and Angles who, like the Norsemen in the western islands, were for a while serious contenders for the domination of the land later named after the Scots who arrived from Ireland in AD 250.

While the Highlands remained for centuries a wild area fought over by fierce rival clans who jealously guarded the glens they controlled, the south and east were by their nature more open to softer foreign influences. The ports and estuaries provided shelter for traders from the south and the intermarriage of Scottish kings with French princesses helped establish cultural interchange which brought about a greater sophistication of manners and customs.

The blossoming of the culture of the Middle Ages, brought about by the contact with the refinements of the East at the time of the Crusades, included the concepts of chivalry and courtly love which gradually changed the rough and ready ways of European courts for the better.

In Scotland, this change is apparent in the literature of the twelfth and thirteenth centuries when anonymous authors put into ballad form some of the existing legends, giving them that romantic and more kindly character that expresses the ideals of the age of chivalry, if not its reality. Many ballads have come down to us from this time, including those about Tam Lin and Thomas the Rhymer (pp. 17 and 42), both of which appear as legends in this book. The romantic ballad had another period of fashionable popularity, when the romantic poets found one of their sources of inspiration in the work of the legendary poet Ossian. Sir Walter Scott who, single-handed, revived many almost lost medieval Scottish ballads, also wrote his own ballads, such as *The Eve of Saint John*, which may have been inspired by memories of legends heard and read in his own childhood.

Thus, many of the legends of the Lowlands and Eastern Scotland as they have come to us, seem less pitiless, less intransigent in their attitudes, than those of the Highlands. Though often violent in subject they lack the unfeeling cruelty of such legends as the story of Iain Dubh of Dunvegan, or the disposal of an unwanted wife by a MacLean of Duart. Only as you near the Highland border do you find that kind of indifference to human feelings demonstrated in this book by the story of the entombed wife of Loch Con (p. 113) and the cruelly treated daughter of Lord Rait (p. 143).

Another striking characteristic of Lowland and East Scottish legends is that they often have a wry sense of humour, as in the story of the burial of the woman of

8

Carrbridge (p. 133) or the description of how a minister of Dunkeld got the better of the devil (p. 100). Both these legends also illustrate the stronger influence of Christianity in the south, for in the first it is the woman's desire of a Christian burial that is the motive for the events of the legend, and in the second the devil is defeated by a Christian's witty solution to a devilish problem.

As in the north, the legends of the south and the east were largely transmitted by word of mouth in communities but perhaps there was a greater dissemination by wandering entertainers and troubadours than in the Highlands where communication was more difficult. Thus the ballads were a form of entertainment for everybody at a court or in a castle and the entertainers tailored their stories to their audiences. This might modify the presentation of the subject matter from one place to another, but it also gave the stories a life and variety all too often lost once the narrative became pinned down in words. It probably also made the stories more real for their audiences, depending as they then did on the storyteller's personal charisma and his skill in making all the events sound convincing. This was an art indeed now largely lost, owing to our dependence on canned entertainment.

Because legends may have many different versions, depending on how many storytellers recounted them, and where they did so, they are sometimes elusive and their detail difficult to pin down, though at their heart there is a truth that is beyond reason, and lays bare the deep subconscious symbolism of a people.

In selecting the stories of Eastern Scotland and the Lowlands for inclusion here, we have tried to include some that are familiar (though their place of origin may not be known to many) and others that may not be so well known but whose settings are usually on the itinerary of most tourists in Scotland. In this way, we hope to add an extra dimension to a familiar journey or to interest readers in visiting a new place through being attracted by its legend.

The stories have come from many sources. Sometimes they have been told to us after we had already read them in some collection of Scottish stories, at other times we heard them first and read them afterwards. The historical stories related are included here because although based on actual events, they have acquired a legendary quality over the years.

At the end of the book we include a list of publications that gave us great pleasure during our researches, while also providing a version – sometimes several versions – of stories we may have been told about or found hinted at in guide books.

The Walks

Most of the walks included in this book have been planned so that they can be undertaken by people of all ages, though children under six will find some of them too long without a piggy-back from a willing dad or friend, or perhaps too hilly to undertake at all. In some cases, the walks were along planned tracks in areas under the authority of the Forestry Commission, or along specified paths planned by local tourist authorities; yet others are along unpaved and unfenced minor roads which make perfectly good walkways since there is little traffic along them; others still take in areas of hill or farmland with no obvious path.

On the walks here we have estimated the approximate distance of the round trip, assuming that you are going to end your walk where you began it. The one or two exceptions are clearly indicated. We have not attempted to be exact because there are often slight alternatives to the path you follow. Nor have we given estimated times for the walks because this will vary from person to person, and according to how often you stop to look at things.

Roughly speaking, you should be able to walk at four miles an hour without too much effort over relatively level ground. For hill walking, the rate may be two to two-and-a-half-miles an hour.

The word 'tracks' needs some explanation. On the Ordnance Survey maps there are ways marked by broken lines which in some cases are fenced but paved roads, and in others open unpaved tracks across a field indicated only by the fact that farm or forestry vehicles use them. In some cases, we have called them 'tracks' to be distinguished from 'paths' by the fact that a track, as we call it, has seemed to us capable of allowing passage for vehicles. In some cases these tracks may simply be access routes across private land.

The map references given for each walk are based on the Ordnance Survey 1:50,000 series and pin-point the starting place.

The footpath system which is such a feature of walks in England hardly exists in Scotland. Broadly speaking, you will either be walking along single-track minor roads or across private land. In many cases, the land is open moorland covered in grass or heather and very inviting for exploratory walks to the tops of hills.

Farmers and landowners do not, on the whole, mind your walking over their land as long as you treat it with the proper respect. Where you have to enter their land near a farm building it is courteous to ask permission to do so. We have never encountered any refusals, but the continued goodwill of those who own and work the land will depend on the behaviour of those who walk over it. Please therefore always make sure that you do not do any damage to fences, that you close gates and that you do not frighten sheep, cattle or other animals that may be within the fenced-in areas. This is particularly important in springtime during the lambing season.

One other note of warning: during the shooting and stalking season certain walks can be dangerous. Inform yourself locally about whether a shoot or stalk is taking place, and avoid the area.

If you enjoy something more than a short stroll around the place where the legend is set, you may be tempted to take off across hillsides to the ever-beckoning horizon. If you do – and this is particularly important on mountainsides cut by steep ravines – remember that the weather in Scotland can change very rapidly. You can be surrounded by thick mist or rain, and in springtime even get caught in a snowstorm, with devastating speed. Always carry a map and compass with you and learn how to use them before you set off in the morning. If you also carry a whistle, and some food, you should be all right on all the walks given here providing your clothing is sensible – and this is vital. Never go wandering in the countryside in Scotland in thin clothes and town sandals. You should always carry a sweater and a waterproof anorak or jacket however hot the day when you start out, and always wear reasonably stout shoes with ridged soles; smooth leather or plastic soles slip on grassy hillsides.

Wherever you walk in southern and eastern Scotland, remember the Country Code:

Guard against all fire risks
Fasten all gates
Keep all dogs under proper control
Avoid disturbing farm stock
Keep to the paths across farm land
Avoid damaging fences, hedges and walls
Leave no litter
Safeguard water supplies
Protect wildlife, wild plants and trees
Go carefully on country roads
Respect the life of the countryside

Travelling around Scotland

We have assumed that you will probably be driving and therefore the walks start near a place where you may park your car. If yo are not travelling by car, you will find that there is a bus service going somewhere near the start of most of the walks, but these services may only be once a day in each direction, so we have decided not to include specific route numbers. Bus timetables can be obtained from the Scottish National Tourist Office in Edinburgh, and from most local tourist offices, where staff can usually advise you on the frequency of services.

The Scottish National Tourist Board's information centres are also very helpful in telling you about what's on in their locality. The National Trust for Scotland, too, has excellent information centres at sites owned by them.

In writing this book and its counterpart *Western Scotland and the Highlands* we have travelled far and wide over Scotland and we have discovered many beautiful places that we had not visited before, as well as more fascinating facts about the places that we already knew.

The result of our research had confirmed in us more than ever the conviction that Scotland has a beauty that never fails to surprise and enthrall and a mystery that bewitches those who take time to be more than just summer tourists.

Wherever we have visited we have been met with courtesy and have discovered something of interest, and we have rarely come across that dourness for which the Scots are reputed.

The accommodation, whether in an old baronial manor or at a humble bed and breakfast, has been exemplary and the elbow grease supplied by Scottish landladies absolutely dazzling.

THE BORDER COUNTRY

1. THOMAS THE RHYMER
The Eildon Hills

The Eildon Hills lie to the south of Melrose, rising abruptly out of the surrounding countryside. The hills are, in fact, the three volcanic peaks of one hill, which legend says was split into three peaks by a devil, who was carrying out a task set him by the wizard, Michael Scot (see p. 162).

The outline of the green Eildon Hills, set against the sky amidst a countryside thick with trees and with the ribbon of the Tweed flowing in front, was a favourite view of Sir Walter Scott, which he never tired of walking up Bemersyde Hill, near Melrose, to see.

The hills are also said to have been a favourite of another medieval figure, Thomas the Rhymer, who was almost a contemporary of Michael Scot, and whose story was recounted in Walter Scott's *Minstrelsy of the Scottish Borders*.

The man who has come down to us in ballad and legend as Thomas the Rhymer was a thirteenth-century poet and prophet named Thomas· Learmont who lived in, and was perhaps born at, the village of Ercildoune (present-day Earlston) near Melrose. He is said to have received his powers of prophecy at the hands of the Queen of Elfland herself.

He had been lying day-dreaming under a tree near a chattering stream, with the outline of the Eildon Hills dominating his view, when the Queen of Elfland came riding by. Her milk-white horse, its mane hung with tiny silver bells which tinkled as it moved, trod delicately over the turf to the Eildon tree, and the green silken skirt of its beautiful rider fluttered in the breeze, allowing a glimpse of a delicate foot shod in a tiny green velvet shoe richly embroidered.

Thomas of Ercildoune was naturally deeply affected by this wonderful and unexpected sight. He leaped to his feet, pulling off his bonnet, and bowed deeply and gracefully. The Queen of Elfland was as much affected by the sight of this handsome young mortal as he had been by her, and instantly resolved to carry him off to Elfland with her.

Soon, Thomas of Ercildoune was kissing the lovely lady's rosy lips under the Eildon Tree, and thus was in thrall to her, for her breath and her lips exerted a magic spell over him. Unresisting, he mounted behind her on her milk-white steed and was carried away with a speed greater than that of the wind over mountain and desert, over land and sea, far from the Eildon Hills and Scotland – far, indeed, from the world we know, to Elfland.

There, the Queen of Elfland held Thomas of Ercildoune captive for seven years. During all this time, he dared not speak a word, for a mortal's voice, if heard in Elfland, would prevent that mortal ever returning to his own country. So Thomas of Ercildoune dressed himself in the elfin clothes of a coat of smooth cloth and green velvet shoes and watched and listened, learning many things about the fairies and their ways, but he spoke not at all.

At the end of seven years, the Queen of Elfland decided that Thomas must return to his own country. For wages, she gave him an apple which, when eaten, would ensure that his tongue could never tell a lie again. At first, Thomas demurred, foreseeing that to be unable ever to utter a lie could well turn out to be a mixed blessing. The Queen was adamant, however, and Thomas took his apple and ate it.

Soon, he was back in the Eildon Hills, to the delight of his friends and family who had long since given him up for dead. Once all the excitement of his homecoming had died away, he wrote a poem recounting the romance of his life in

Elfland which brought him recognition as a poet and earned him the name 'Thomas the Rhymer'. Soon he became famous throughout Scotland as a prophet as well, for the Queen of Elfland's gift of a tongue which could not lie translated itself on earth into an ability to prophesy the future.

He is said to have foreseen Alexander III's death, which was a great blow to the political and social stability of Scotland. In March 1286, Thomas the Rhymer remarked to friends as they sat under the Eildon tree that 'on the morrow, afore noon, shall blow the greatest wind that ever was heard before in Scotland'. The following day, Alexander III was killed when his horse bolted with him and plunged over a steep cliff on the Fife coast.

He once wrote:

> York was, London is and Edinburgh shall be
> The biggest and bonniest of the three,

a sentiment which many would say is already true of the latter quality, even if not of the former.

During the rest of his earthly life, Thomas the Rhymer lived outwardly the life of an ordinary country gentleman in his tower castle at Ercildoune. He married and had children. He wrote poetry, entertained his friends, and saw to the business of his estate; but he never forgot the fairy folk of Elfland, and they never entirely lost their hold on him, a hold which seemed at its strongest on the occasions when he would sit under the Eildon Tree and issue his prophecies.

One evening, when he was nearing his seventy-eighth year, he sat dining in some state and with much merriment, surrounded by his guests, in the great hall of his castle. Suddenly, a servant ran into the hall in considerable panic. A doe and a hind had come out of the forest, had followed him all the way up the village street and were even now stamping their hooves on the ground outside Thomas of Ercildoune's gate. The prophet rose to his feet, bowed to his friends, and walked out of his castle, to follow the doe and the hind back down the village street and into the forest. He was never seen again, though many people said for generations afterwards that he still frequented Earth. He might be seen helping the fairies in some task, or buying horses for the sleeping warriors who live in a cave under the Eildon Hills. Perhaps he is still there.

The Eildon Tree has long since vanished, but a stone by the roadside a mile east of Melrose marks the spot where it stood. A little further away, the Bogle Burn, named after the Goblins with whom Thomas Rhymer was supposed to converse, tumbles into the Tweed just before it bends round to flow beneath Scott's View on Bemersyde Hill.

THE WALK:	MAP SQUARE:
FROM THE TOWN SQUARE IN MELROSE, THROUGH THE EILDON HILLS AND NEWSTEAD BACK TO MELROSE.	Ordnance Survey Sheet 73/548340 A 4-mile walk taking in major places of interest in the area of the Eildon Hills.

Our SUGGESTED WALK round Melrose and the Eildon Hills is based on the walk planned by the Melrose Tourist Information Department and the Borders Regional Council Tourist Information Department for the use of visitors, and which is available as a pamphlet from the Tourist Information Centre at Melrose. This attractive Border town, with its famous abbey, lies two miles west of the main A68(T), and is easily reached by car, or by public transport, as there are regular and frequent bus services between Melrose and other towns of the Border Region.

The walk begins in Melrose Square, which lies just to the south of the abbey. Leave the square by the B6359, signposted

The Eildon Hills.

Lilliesleaf, and cross under the track of the now dismantled railway line. At the first signpost on the left-hand side of the road, you will see a flight of steps which you climb down. At the bottom, you cross the bridge over the stream which flows north past the abbey in Melrose, then climb up again to another stile which you cross into a field on the lower slopes of the highest Eildon Hills.

Keeping to the hedge on the right-hand edge of the field, you carry on uphill (not too steeply), passing through a gate and over a stile into the next field, where the path now follows the left-hand edge to another stile.

At this point, rather less than three-quarters of a mile from the beginning of your walk, you will start to climb more steeply along the western slopes of Eildon Hill North, and walkers who want to avoid this should turn left over the stile here and follow the lower path which skirts the lower slopes of the hill.

For those carrying on, the path climbs via heather- and gorse-covered slopes to the saddle between the two larger Eildons. From here, you will see a wide path turning left to the summit of Eildon Hill North (1,313 feet).

The Romans used this summit as a signal station and lookout point, since it commanded such extensive views all round. Before them, the early Britons had had a fort here, remains of which may still be seen just below the summit. We hope it will be a clear day for you, because the views from the summit can be spectacular, taking in Melrose, the broad, sweeping ribbon of the Tweed and, to the south, the Cheviot Hills.

From the summit, you follow the path down the eastern slopes of the hill, coming to a stile where your path and the path along the lower slopes join up again – a good point at which to meet up with any of your party who may have elected to follow the less steep route.

From the stile, the path takes you through a copse of trees to the main road (the A6091), where you turn right (unless you want to go back to Melrose at this point, in which case, you turn left and follow the road back to town, a distance of about three-quarters of a mile).

Having turned right, cross the road and walk to a track sign-posted 'The Eildon Walk' and going off to the left. Follow this under the railway to a T-junction in Newstead village, which is said to be the oldest inhabited place in Scotland and where the stonemasons who built Melrose Abbey lived.

At the T-junction take the path to the left which leads on to the road. (The right-hand path goes into Newstead village and leads to the site of the great Roman Fort of Trimontium, three-quarters of a mile from the village.)

Your route, which is now a narrow path, leads behind a group of bungalows along the embankment and into a council housing estate. You will come to a gap in the houses bearing right; follow this, cross a bridge, and you will find yourself in the park next to Melrose Abbey. At the National Trust for Scotland shop and information centre near the abbey, you turn left to reach Melrose Square and the end of the walk.

2. THE WORME OF LINTON
Linton

Linton parish lies close to the Border in Roxburghshire, south-east of Kelso. This is quiet and peaceful farming country today, a land of gentle hills watered by many streams, wooded with copses and coverts of fine trees, and dotted with pretty hamlets.

The village of Linton, with Linton Hill rising a thousand feet behind it to the north, is now no more than a house or two and the parish church, which sits on a sandy knoll to the west of the B6436.

Four or five centuries ago, things were not so quiet, for Linton, placed so near the Border, was on a recognized raiders' route through the Cheviot Hills and was often plundered and wrecked during the incessant Scots versus English warfare of the times.

Before this, sometime during the twelfth century, Linton had had an even nastier problem to cope with – a giant Worme or dragon.

The creature had its lair in a cave near the village: a cave on the north-east side of Linton Hill on the edge of Greenlees Farm is today credited with being the site, and is marked as such on the sketch map in the printed parish history. From this 'worm's hole' the creature would issue forth to steal itself a sheep or cow, and greatly frightened the local people.

As more and more of Linton's population fled to the safety of Kelso or Jedburgh, so the rumours about the Worme grew. Naturally, no one wished to belittle his own courage by letting people think that he had fled an insignificant dog or wolf, or bear. So the Worme got bigger. From being a few feet long and the thickness of a man's arm, the Worme grew to twelve feet and the size of a tree trunk. Soon, it was long enough and strong enough to be able to coil itself round a small hill called Wormiston.

As it grew, so it became more fierce. Its breath was so venomous that it could kill animals yards away, and its great fangs could draw them in without the Worme's having to drag its whole length from its cave. For some distance round the cave, the trees and grass had been scorched by the Worme's fiery breath, and its terrifying snorts and grunts kept people several miles away awake at night, shuddering with fright behind locked and bolted doors.

A few bolder spirits had tried to kill the Worme, but their arrows, spears, and slung stones had merely recoiled from its scaly body.

Then came the young knight, Somerville of Lariston, upon the scene. His family possessed lands near Linton, but he himself had been away for some time and had known nothing of the Worme until chance brought word of it to him. He instantly resolved to return to Linton and slay the creature.

As soon as he arrived, he stayed only to don his armour, polished by his page until it gleamed in the sunlight, and to test his lance with the pennant fluttering gaily from it, before mounting his horse and sallying forth to deal bravely with the Worme.

The creature, alerted to Somerville's approach by the pounding of his horse's hooves on the turf, uncoiled itself from its lair and rose up, glaring at the young knight with its great jaw gaping open. Somerville of Lariston couched his lance and charged full tilt at the Worme. The lance broke against the monster's shoulder and Somerville himself was lucky to escape the dreadful fangs and horrid steaming breath of the creature.

Undaunted, he remounted his horse and rode away to think. Clearly, ordinary weapons would not do. Soon an idea came to him. From what other people told him, it seemed that the Worme always held its jaw gaping wide open when approaching anyone, as it had done with himself. What if Somerville could thrust a large chunk of material – peat perhaps – soaked in hot pitch and impaled on his lance, down the creature's throat? Surely the pitch fumes would suffocate it, while the chunk of peat would stop the creature's venomous breath from issuing forth and killing the knight.

The next day, clad once more in his shining armour and with a new lance in his hand, the knight went forth again to confront the Worme. His page accompanied him, bearing a pot of steaming hot pitch and a large piece of peat. They came to the Worme's cave and as they waited for it to appear, the page thrust the peat into the hot pitch.

Subterranean rumblings and the hot wind of the Worme's breathing heralded its approach and the knight impaled the peat soaked with the scalding pitch on the end of his lance and held it ready. As the dreadful creature emerged into the daylight, its head turning round to obtain a sight of the man who was daring to molest it again, its jaw stretched wide open. Somerville clapped spurs into his horse's sides and charged forward. Carefully he aimed his lance's point, and pushed it deep down the red-lined throat.

The Worme lashed and twisted in a frenzy, its great coils tightening round Wormiston Hill and making indentations on its sides which may be seen to this day, but it could not choke up the peat. Soon, it lay suffocated and silent on the ground.

Thus was Linton rid of its great Worme.

To show their gratitude, the villagers of Linton called on one of the foremost sculptors of the day to make a memorial stone depicting the knight killing the Worme, and they placed it prominently in their parish church, over the west door, where it may still be seen. Somerville was also given land in Linton, where later generations of the family built themselves a tower castle on the mound south-east of the church, looking out over Kale Water. It was destroyed by the English in 1523.

THE WALK:
FROM LINTON PARISH CHURCH THROUGH THE VILLAGE AND UP LINTON HILL.

MAP SQUARE:
Ordnance Survey Sheet 74/773262
A 4-mile walk round the gentle farmland of Linton.

Linton lies six miles south-east of Kelso and a mile north of Morebattle on the B6436, on the edge of the valley carved out of the hills by Kale Water on its journey west to the River Teviot.

Linton Parish Church.

To find the parish church, drive to Linton on the B6436 (the road is signposted 'Morebattle' out of Kelso). You will pass Linton Farm on your left, and a few hundred yards further on is the right-hand turning to the parish church.

The church stands on a sandy knoll, and has no obvious solid foundations – an architectural wonder which has itself inspired a legend of how the knoll came to be there and how the church was built. (A young man killed a priest here and was condemned to death. His two sisters, interceding on his behalf, were told they could save his life if they sifted sufficient sand to form a mound on which to build a church. They completed this herculean task – though one of the sisters died immediately afterwards – the church was built and the young man's life saved.)

Inside the church you will find several objects of interest, including the Norman font, seventeenth-century oak stalls, and the coats of arms of the four families who held the patronage of Linton.

Outside, the main object of interest must be the stone tympanum above the church door. The sandstone sculpture here, obviously Norman and unique in Scotland, has weathered surprisingly well the eight centuries since it was carved and its subject is still clear. It is a knight on horseback and with a falcon on his shoulder thrusting his lance down on a creature which – alas for the legend! – seems to be four-footed and more like a bear or a wolf than a dragon. The sculpture is now set behind glass to preserve it from the elements.

Having seen the church and perhaps deciphered the inscriptions on the gravestones round the church, you can walk back towards the village – or what remains of it – to climb Linton Hill.

Leaving the church, turn left again at the road and walk back past Linton Farm. Ignoring the track up to the covert a hundred yards or so past Linton Farm, take the minor road marked 'Bankhead' and 'Greenlees' which is the next turning on the right.

A couple of hundred yards past the main buildings of Bankhead Farm, you will notice a small burn flowing down from Linton Hill (over the fence to your right). This offers an easy route, hilly rather than steep, up to the summit of the hill, from where you may obtain some fine views of the surrounding parishes. As this is farming land, you should ask permission from the farmer before starting out; he will be concerned only that you remember to close any gates behind you, and not trample down his fences.

The route from the church to the top of Linton Hill is two miles long. The walk up Linton Hill from the farm is considerably shorter, of course – well under a mile, and you can leave your car in the road by the farm.

3.   THE EVE OF SAINT JOHN
Smailholm Tower, near Melrose

From his earliest childhood, Walter Scott grew to love the
legends and stories of Scotland's Border country. When he
was only three he went to stay with his grandparents at the
farm they rented at Sandyknowe, between Melrose and
Kelso. He learnt many stories of Border history from his
grandmother, and read many more for himself, while
Smailholm Tower, rising above the farm on its 680-feet
rock escarpment, provided him with a near-perfect
example of the kind of Border keep occupied by the bold
knights and barons of medieval times.

Just to climb the steep and rocky path to the tower on its
high crag was spur enough for the boy's imagination. He
would sit and watch the breeze ruffle the surface of Eden
Water below the tower, or look beyond to Dryburgh
Abbey and the Eildon Hills to the west, Hume Castle to
the east and the Cheviots to the south, in his mind
peopling the whole beautiful landscape with stirring
events from the past.

Sandyknowe Farm and Smailholm Tower were the
property of Hugh Scott of Harden, and Walter Scott was
staying at Scott of Harden's home, Mertoun House, in
1799 when he heard that Smailholm was to be demolished.
Scott pleaded for it to be spared, and Scott of Harden
agreed – provided Walter write a ballad about it.

Thus *The Eve of Saint John* came to be written. It was
among Scott's earliest works, and was published in Kelso in
1800, two years before *The Minstrelsy of the Scottish
Border*. The ballad was a romance of guilty love, murder
and revenge, overlaid with the supernatural.

Smailholm Tower.

The Baron of Smaylho'me had been away, supposedly fighting in a Border battle against the English, when he returned unexpectedly to Smaylho'me Tower on St John's Eve. He was still dressed for war, signs of battle sat upon his garb, and his dagger and battle axe were still stained with blood – 'and it was not English gore'.

When he reached Smaylho'me, the Baron dismounted and – instead of going immediately to seek out his wife – whistled for his young page, English Will. When the lad stood before him, the Baron asked him to recount everything that he had seen the Lady of Smaylho'me do during his absence.

Will described how his Lady, three nights before, despite the fact that the wind had been wild and shrill, had left Smalho'me Tower and climbed the steep path to the Watchfold crag, on which a beacon flared, warning the countryside against the English. She had stayed there some time alone in the night, before returning to the tower.

The following night she had repeated the steep walk and this time an armed knight had been awaiting her. The page had watched as, their faces lit by the flames of the beacon, the two had talked long and earnestly, but he had been unable to hear their conversation, so loud had been the wind and so heavy the rain.

The third night, however, the page did hear something of the conversation between the Lady and the knight. She named the midnight hour of St John's Eve, and told the knight to come to her then in her bower. He was not to worry about the Baron, as he was away fighting with the bold Buccleuch, nor need he worry about being discovered coming into Smaylho'me at midnight. She would unlock the tower gate, chain the bloodhound, and strew rushes on the stairs to her bower, so that no one might hear him.

The knight demurred, saying that he dared not come to her; on the Eve of St John he must wander alone. But the lady insisted.

> The night air is sweet, and when lovers meet
> 'Tis worth the whole summer's day . . .
> I conjure thee, my love, to be there!

Still the knight seemed reluctant, saying that he could not pass the priest's room on so guilty an errand. The Lady swept aside this argument, too, telling the knight that the priest had been called to Dryburgh to say masses over three days for the soul of a knight who had been slain.

Finally, Will told the Baron, the knight had agreed to meet the Lady in her tower, though he still showed little enthusiasm for the tryst, saying that the priest may as well be saying a mass for his soul, too.

The Baron, red-faced with jealous fury, demanded to know the knight's name, but when the page told him 'Sir Richard of Coldinghame', his colour changed to a deathly pallor. He knew – none better! – that Sir Richard of Coldinghame was dead, slain by some secret foe full three nights before. Even now, the black monks of Dryburgh were singing for Sir Richard of Coldinghame.

That night, both the Baron and his Lady slept ill. The Baron tossed and turned and muttered to himself, as if for reassurance, 'his bloody grave is deep – It cannot give up the dead!' Eventually, towards dawn, he fell into a heavy slumber and so did not see the last meeting between his fair Lady and her lover, Sir Richard of Coldinghame.

When the time came for the tryst the Lady had so eagerly awaited, it was a spirit who stood before her in her bower. Sir Richard of Coldinghame told her:

> By the Eildon Tree, for long nights three
> In bloody grave I have lain;
> The mass and dead prayers are said for me,
> But, Lady, they are said in vain!

The Lady, trembling, asked what he meant – was he saved, or lost? For answer, he laid one hand on an oak stand, reached out with the other and touched her wrist. The Lady shrank away from him and fainted, for the touch was fiery.

The black scorch marks of his fingers remained impressed for ever on the oak, and evermore that Lady wore a covering on her wrist.

Sir Richard was dead, his restless spirit doomed to dwell

on the beacon's crag. As for the Baron and his fair and faithless Lady:

> There is a nun in Melrose bower,
> Who ne'er looks to the Sun;
> There is a Monk in Dryburgh Tower,
> He speaketh word to none.

Thus all three characters in the drama assuaged their guilt.

| THE WALK: | MAP SQUARE: |
| FROM MELROSE ABBEY TO DRYBURGH ABBEY. | Ordnance Survey Sheet 73/548342 A 4½-mile walk along country roads, linking two great Border abbeys. |

As Smailholm Tower is more readily accessible by car than by walking, there being no good walking paths to the area, we have decided to suggest as the walk here the road route between the abbeys in which two of the protagonists in the tale ended their days. This is very much Scott country, and the walk will take you to places closely associated with him. The novelist is, of course, buried in Dryburgh Abbey, and you may see his last resting-place in the abbey church by the north transept.

The walk begins at Melrose Abbey, which was founded by David I in 1136. The buildings of the abbey were destroyed on numerous occasions in its history, though sufficient remains to give a good idea of its original size and layout. Michael Scot is supposed to be buried here.

From the abbey, you take the Jedburgh road out of Melrose. This is the A6091 which lies a block to the south of the abbey. After a few hundred yards, you will come to a minor road forking left to Newstead. Follow this under the railway line through Newstead, then up to Leaderfoot (about one and three-quarter miles from Melrose), where you cross the Tweed. Once over the bridge, you turn right on to the minor road to Bemersyde Hill and the famous viewpoint, Scott's View, one and a half miles from Leaderfoot.

The walk along this stretch of road is pretty, and the views from Bemersyde Hill (741 feet) and Scott's View are superb, with the Eildon Hills rising beyond the Tweed and the wooded countryside in between. From Scott's View, you continue along the road south until you reach a T-junction, where you turn right. Where the road bends left to continue south towards Dryburgh Abbey, a mile away, the large house set off the road on the right is Bemersyde House, seat of the Haig family, one of whose more illustrious sons was the World War I general, Earl Haig, now buried at Dryburgh.

You will find the abbey, set in lovely parkland within a loop of the River Tweed, through the village of Dryburgh. Like Melrose, this abbey was founded in the reign of David I, probably by the Constable of Scotland, Hugh de Morville; also like Melrose, it was destroyed and rebuilt several times in the course of its history.

NB. An alternative route from Melrose to Dryburgh, which is shorter and cuts out much of the road walking, though it also cuts out Scott's View, is to take the path east out of Newstead to Ravenswood (instead of the road to Leaderfoot); from here you follow the bank of the Tweed past Newtown St Boswells to where a footbridge takes you across to Dryburgh just west of the abbey.

4. THE GHOST THAT DANCED AT JETHART
Jedburgh

Jedburgh in Roxburghshire lies to the south of Teviotdale, just ten miles north of the Border. Originally called Jethart, it was the most important of the Border towns and played an important part in Border history. Its castle, long since destroyed, stood on the site of the present castellated prison, but ruins of the Abbey, which was built about the same time as the castle and was also one of the strong points of the town, still remain. Jedburgh and its fighting men were much feared over the Border and their cry of 'Jetharts here!' was enough to send their enemies scattering. Like many a frontier town of more recent years Jedburgh had a rough system of justice which often meant that justice was meted out even before a trial was held.

The Abbey, which is best seen from the banks of the Jed river, was founded by David I around 1138 and has always had a close connection with the Scottish kings and queens. By the time that Mary Queen of Scots came to Jedburgh in 1566, however, the Abbey had already been destroyed by Henry VIII in a fit of pique because Mary's Scottish advisers were against her marriage to his son Edward. The house in which Mary lived still stands in the town and can be visited (March to October, daily 10.00–17.30). It was from here that Mary made her famous ride to Bothwell's bedside at Hermitage Castle, where he lay wounded; on her return, the Queen fell seriously ill and nearly died at Jedburgh.

There is another story of ill-omen about a Scottish king in Jedburgh which is as well known as that of Queen Mary's ride. This time, the setting is Jedburgh Abbey. The date is 1285 and Alexander III is celebrating his second marriage.

Alexander's first marriage to Margaret, daughter of Henry III of England, ended with her death in 1275. Ten years later on 14 October 1285 Alexander married Yolande, daughter of Robert Count of Dreux. A grand banquet in the hall of the Abbey marked the ceremony. The entire Scottish court attended the event and the tables were laden with haunches of venison, game birds, stuffed boars' heads and other delicacies.

Musicians with pipes, string instruments and drums played music for dancing in the hall, and the guests went through the formal figures by the flickering light of the many torches which lit the splendid scene.

The high point of the evening was a procession of maskers who wended their way among the guests singing and dancing and adding to the general mirth and high spirits. Everybody's mind was set on enjoyment and so was unprepared for what happened next. Suddenly, there appeared among the dancers a tall, spectral figure which instantly captured everyone's attention. It was a skeleton whose bones were surrounded by a pale white luminosity which gave it body. From the sockets of its eyes a strange light glowed. The dreadful figure moved slowly among the maskers and guests, who, as it passed among them, crowded fearfully back on each other. The music came jerkily to a stop and there was complete silence in the vast hall. Mesmerized, everyone watched the spectre walk up to the King's table, pause for a moment, and then weave its way once more through the crowd and out of the room.

After this visitation, it was impossible for the festivities to continue. Although the King, quickly recovering his composure, ordered the musicians to play, the guests faded away, and soon the great hall was empty, leaving the bright torches to light abandoned wine and untouched food.

No one could guess the significance of the ghostly visit, but the incident hung like a dark omen over the King whose reign had hitherto been peaceful, bringing a quiet prosperity to Scotland.

Not long after his interrupted wedding festivities, the King set off in March 1286 on a journey from Edinburgh to Kinghorn on the north side of the Firth of Forth. As he rode along with his companions, no thought of the apparition at Jedburgh crossed his mind. Indeed, he had entirely forgotten about it. He was happy. His marriage was a success and had helped to establish good relations with his French relatives. In addition, Edward I of England was preoccupied with his Welsh wars and for the moment did not present a threat to Scotland.

Trotting along the cliffs, King Alexander III of Scotland felt satisfied with the hand destiny had dealt him. Suddenly, as so often happens, tragedy struck. His horse, a normally quiet and well-behaved animal, reared up as if it had seen an apparition and set off at a headlong gallop along the cliff. Try as he would, Alexander could not control him. The horse's hooves pounded along the grassy verge of the cliff, dangerously close to the edge; inevitably, it lost its footing, precipitating itself and its rider into the air and onto the rocks below.

The death of Alexander III was a blow to Scotland. The two sons of his first marriage were dead and his new wife had not presented him with an heir, so there was no one to succeed but his baby granddaughter, Margaret. At first it seemed that she might be betrothed to the son of Edward I and thus unite peacefully the interests of the English and Scottish crowns but it was not to be. Margaret died and her death ended the hopes of peace and ushered in many generations of Border warfare between Scotland and England.

THE WALKS:

MAP SQUARE:

1. FROM CASTLEGATE IN JEDBURGH TO THE FOOT OF DUNION HILL AND BACK TO JEDBURGH.

1. Ordnance Survey Sheet 74/650205

2. FROM JEDBURGH ABBEY VIA FERNIE-HURST CASTLE TO THE CAPON TREE AND BACK TO JEDBURGH.

2. Ordnance Survey Sheet 74/650204

Two easy walks in the vicinity of Jedburgh town.

Jedburgh is the terminus of a branch line off the Berwick-on-Tweed–Edinburgh railway line. The town lies on the A68(T) which runs parallel to the old Roman road, Dere Street, on which the traces of several Roman camps may still be seen. The A698 from Berwick-upon-Tweed to Hawick runs slightly to the north of Jedburgh along the Teviot valley.

Jedburgh is used to visitors and caters for them well. The large well-organized Scottish Tourist Information Office, which is very helpful to visitors, is open all year and has a good selection of guides, maps, and books on sale. The staff can help find accommodation and give advice on things to see and do.

There are several good walks in the vicinity, many of which climb the surrounding hills to give good views of the attractive grey stone town. You can walk along the Roman road. It is accessible from several points, perhaps the easiest being at Jedfoot two miles north of Jedburgh, where there is a well-preserved section of Dere Street.

The FIRST SUGGESTED WALK in Jedburgh is about three miles long and goes to the foot of Dunnion Hill, to the south-west of the town. This walk starts at Castlegate, which is the main street running south-west off the Market Place in the centre of the town. At the top of Castlegate, turn left in front of Jedburgh Castle. This is not the old castle, but a building erected as a jail in 1823 and now the county museum (open April to September, weekdays and Sunday afternoons).

Your walk is now taking you downhill across gently sloping country, with the River Jed below on your left. You cross a footbridge over a burn which flows into the Jed and then walk uphill through a wood for a few hundred yards to Todlaw Farm.

Once through Todlaw Farm, take the first turning on the right off the metalled road and follow the footpath uphill and through more pleasantly wooded country. After about half a mile, having skirted Dunnion Hill and the golf course, you will bear right on to the B6358. The walk back into town along this road is about three-quarters of a mile.

Jedburgh Abbey.

Our SECOND SUGGESTED WALK in Jedburgh (just over three miles in length), takes in three famous sites in the town. Begin at Jedburgh Abbey, which you will probably have just visited (open all year, weekdays and Sunday afternoons).

From the Abbey, walk south and cross the River Jed via the A68 road bridge. Pass the Parish Church, then Inchbonny House which has connections with Walter Scott. Just past the cottage, about half a mile from the start of the walk, turn left on a minor road going south. Walk along here for three-quarters of a mile, then turn right (the first turning to the right you will come to on this road) on to a path which takes you past a row of cottages to Ferniehurst Castle, now a Youth Hostel.

Past the castle, the road is metalled once more and soon brings you out on to the A68. Turn right for the way back to Jedburgh. After a quarter of a mile you will come to the Capon Tree, an ancient oak said to be at least a thousand years old and which may once have been the local hanging tree. From here, the mile-long stretch back to the starting point of the walk follows the A68, crossing the Jed just past the Capon Tree.

Both these walks are based on those planned by the Jedburgh Community Council. A pamphlet describing them and giving a sketch map, is obtainable from most bookshops and stationers in the town, as well as from the Information Office.

5. TAM LIN
Carterhaugh, near Selkirk

Roxburghshire lies along the Border with England. It is a wild and beautiful country with woods and deep valleys where the streams are filled with trout and salmon. The Romans knew the area well and evidence of their presence remains in the vestiges of streets and camps scattered over the hills. In the north runs the River Teviot which joins the Tweed at the town of Kelso, and in the south are the Cheviot Hills, for centuries a much contested area between Scots and English.

In this lonely land, there was once at Carterhaugh a castle in which lived an earl whose daughter, Janet, having reached a romantic age, had taken to strolling about the countryside and day-dreaming the hours away. One day, as she was walking through the woods admiring the wild roses that had just begun to bloom, she was tempted to pluck a white rose which she placed on her bodice. She was so engrossed in this task that she hardly noticed that a young man had suddenly appeared from behind a bush and was examining her closely.

When he spoke, she looked up with a start, not only because his voice had taken her by surprise but because it upbraided her for having taken the rose. There was no way in which she could replace the rose on the bush so she fingered it nervously wondering what to do. Then the young man smiled and explained that he was the guardian of the roses and that it was his job to protect them from strangers who might try to pick them. Janet felt relieved to hear the friendly tone of his voice and surprised when he suddenly plucked a red rose and offered it to her, so that she could add it to the white one.

'I thought,' she said mockingly, 'that you were not supposed to do that.'

'I'm not,' he replied. 'Except for you.'

Janet looked at the young man carefully; she was not used to the company of men and she was still feeling rather nervous, so to cover her confusion she asked him his name.

'Tam Lin,' he said, and a shiver of alarm went through her. Tam Lin was known locally to be an elf and she was afraid of being caught in some magic spell that might turn her into a wild creature or whisk her away for ever to the subterranean places where the faeries lived.

'Don't worry,' Tam Lin said, as if he had read her thoughts. 'I am really a human being, but one day when I was out hunting with my father, the Earl of Roxburgh, I fell behind the hunting party and was kidnapped by the faery queen. I'd do anything to get back to being a human again.'

Janet knew then that the most important thing in her life had suddenly become the wish to rescue Tam Lin from the faery queen. But how could she, a mere mortal, succeed against the magic power of the faeries?

'It is like this,' Tam Lin said. 'There is only one night in the year when it can be done and that is Hallowe'en, which is tonight. All the faeries, witches and other supernatural creatures will be riding out at midnight and it is then that you must grab me off my horse and not let go whatever happens.'

Though terrified at the prospect of facing the power of the faery queen and her people, Janet determined that she would rescue Tam Lin whatever happened. Just before midnight she walked along the path to the spot where she had met Tam Lin and hid herself among the wild roses. She did not have to wait long before she heard the sound of horses' hooves and the faery procession came into view.

The dazzling light almost blinded her but she kept her eyes closely on every person who rode by as she tried to spot Tam Lin.

Above the slow sound of the hooves she could hear the strains of the pipes and, every now and again, the rushing wind of the witches and other creatures of the air as they swooped among the trees. Janet was afraid that she would be discovered before Tam Lin came in sight but the others were too preoccupied with their procession to look for hidden strangers. Suddenly, the music grew louder and a troupe of dancing creatures of the underworld came by, playing their pipes and drums and calling out the name of the faery queen. Janet looked on amazed as the queen rode by. She almost forgot to take note of those around the queen, but not quite. Suddenly, there was Tam Lin looking pale and handsome on a white horse in the midst of the crowd.

Leaping out of the rose bush, Janet hurled herself at him with a cry that startled the faery throng and clasped her arms round his waist.

'He's mine!' she shouted above the confusion as the horses wheeled and stamped and the faeries cried out in alarm. The faery queen was looking at her with blazing eyes but Janet hung on – though what she was now hanging on to was not Tam Lin's warm waist but the scaly belly of a reptile. Remembering what Tam Lin had told her, she dug her nails into the creature's sides as it wriggled to get away. Now the creature was winding itself about her like a giant snake, choking the breath out of her but still she hung on. Then, when she thought she was about to expire, the body of Tam Lin became a rod of burning iron which seared her clothes and burnt her flesh but still Janet refused to give in.

Janet's determination won over even the faery queen. With an imperious gesture, abruptly she returned Tam

Lin to his earthly shape, as naked as the day he had been born and then, with a malicious smile, waved her faery band on.

Her eyes shining with triumph, Janet removed her cloak and covered Tam Lin and then took his hand and escorted him back to the castle of Carterhaugh to tell her father her strange story.

THE WALK:	MAP SQUARE:
A CHOICE OF FARMLAND AND WOODLAND WALKS IN THE BEAUTIFUL YARROW VALLEY, BASED ON THE BOWHILL ESTATE.	Ordnance Survey Sheet 73/427279 Easy walks at will.

Carterhaugh, scene of the legend of Tam Lin, may be reached by road from Selkirk, the nearest big town, which is only two miles away. For a pleasant drive out of Selkirk which allows a view of Carterhaugh before the start of the walk, take the B7009 (the Ettrickbridge road) south out of the town, and turn right off it on to the B7039, the road to the Yarrow Valley. This crosses Ettrick Water by a small bridge at a point where the picturesque river is lined with trees.

Once over the bridge, turn right, still on the B7039. After about half a mile you will pass the turning to Carterhaugh Farm, but as our SUGGESTED WALK here brings you to the farm anyway, there is no need to stop at this point. Continue along the B7039 for another mile until you reach the well-sign-posted turning for the Bowhill estate, which is where the walk begins.

Bowhill, the seat of the Duke of Buccleuch, has been in the possession of the Scotts of Buccleuch for many generations, though the present house dates from 1795. It contains a superb collection of French furniture and many fine paintings by famous artists, including Leonardo da Vinci, Van Dyck, Gainsborough, Reynolds and Canaletto, so you will probably want to visit it (open daily, May to September) before going for a walk through the estate.

In the grounds, nature trails have been laid out to allow visitors to discover the beauties of the countryside here, which, as the estate lies between Yarrow Water and Ettrick Water, are considerable.

To reach Carterhaugh Farm from Bowhill, follow the track which skirts the western edge of the lake south of the house. This goes south through a stretch of delightful woodland, a mixture of conifers, birch, and shrubs, until it reaches first the fields then the extensive outbuildings of the farm, about a mile from Bowhill.

6. THE WICKED DEEDS AND TERRIBLE END OF LORD SOULIS
Hermitage Castle, Liddesdale

A castle was first built by Hermitage Water in Liddesdale in the mid-thirteenth century. The fortunes of war ensured that Hermitage and Liddesdale changed hands with bewildering frequency in the fourteenth century as first Scots, then English, lords held it as a Border fortress. During this time it was largely rebuilt, so that the present massive, square, imposing structure standing gaunt and solitary on the bleak moorland, differs considerably from what it was like in its early days, when the powerful de Soulis family, hereditary King's Butlers (or Seneschals) of Scotland, built and fortified it.

Hermitage Castle.

In 1342 it was occupied by Sir William Douglas, the famous Knight of Liddesdale, who seized his enemy, Sir Alexander Ramsay, and starved him to death in a pit in the castle's dungeon. Ramsay is said to have survived his cruel confinement for seventeen days, living on grains of corn which trickled through from the granary above. At the end of the fifteenth century, the castle became the property of the Hepburns, Earls of Bothwell, and it was there that James, fourth Earl of Bothwell, lying wounded after a Border foray, was visited by Mary Queen of Scots in October 1566. She rode to her lover from Jedburgh and back in one day – a distance of some fifty miles over bleak and dangerous moorland – a ride which nearly killed her and caused much scandal.

Even these wild deeds fade to insignificance beside the activities of William, Lord Soulis. He was the last of his family to hold Hermitage, for he joined a conspiracy against Robert the Bruce in 1320 but was discovered and thrown into Dumbarton Castle, where he died – or so the history books say.

Local folk knew differently, however, and many tales were passed down from one generation to the next about the wicked Lord Soulis and the manner of his death. Walter Scott's friend, John Leyden, the Denholm poet, was sufficiently attracted by these tales to write two ballads about them, based partly on legend and partly on known facts.

One of Lord Soulis's wicked deeds involved the murder of a strong and brave knight from Tynedale, who may have been Sir Richard Knout of Kielder, who died around 1290. Leyden's ballad about him, *The Cout of Keeldar*, was very popular in its day. (Cout, meaning 'colt', was indicative of the knight's strength and boldness.)

The Cout of Keilder (to give him the spelling used in place names at Hermitage) went out in his magic armour and with a band of retainers to seek out the Lord Soulis in his grim fastness at Hermitage. He told his wife that he intended going hunting in Liddesdale, but she, not believing him, warned him to beware of Soulis's strength. Even Lord Soulis's familiar spirit, Old Redcap, appeared to warn the Cout against going any further, but the Cout was sure that his magic armour would protect him even if the presence of his retainers proved insufficient to hold Soulis in check.

Arriving at Hermitage, Keilder had sufficient premonition of trouble to warn his retainers to keep their wits about them and their daggers close to hand, ready to plunge with unerring speed into the enemies' breasts at the first hint of anything untoward.

Lord Soulis appeared smiling and welcoming at the great gate of his castle, and invited the Cout of Kielder and his men to enter and feast with him.

The revelry went on for many hours, and there was much singing and revelry. Then –

> Sudden the tapers cease to burn,
>   The ministrels cease to play . . .
>
> Each hunter bold, of Keeldar's train
>   Sat an enchanged man;
> For cold as ice, through every vein,
>   The freezing life-blood ran
>
> Each rigid hand the whinger wrung,
>   Each gazed with glaring eyes;
> But Keeldar from the table sprung,
>   Unharm'd by gramarye.

The Cout's magic armour enabled him to break free of Soulis's encircling ruffians and their lances, and he gained the open air. It seemed as if he might escape from Liddesdale altogether, but Old Redcap advised Soulis to tell his men to use their lances to force the knight towards Hermitage Water and hold him under with their weapons, 'for no spell can stay the living tide'.

Thus was the brave Cout of Keilder drowned. He was buried near Hermitage Chapel, which stood upstream from the castle,

> Where weep the birches with branches green,
>> Without the holy ground,
> Between two old grey stones is seen
>> The warrior's ridgy mound.

As it was in Leyden's day, so it is now, and visitors may still see a green mound outside the chapel's burial ground which is said to mark the spot of his grave. The Cout of Keilder Pool may also be seen in Hermitage Water.

Lord Soulis's own death was even more dreadful than that of the Cout. Several attempts were made to assassinate him, but he was found to be impervious to lances or spears. He himself was unconcerned at these efforts to kill him, as Redcap had told him that nothing his enemies tried against him would be successful, 'till threefold ropes of sifted sand around thy body twine'.

In the end, his enemies having consulted the writings of Michael Scot and Thomas the Rhymer, did indeed bind him with ropes of sand, then wrapped him in a sheet of lead and boiled him in a brazen cauldron on the Nine Stane Rig until he melted, bones, lead and all. They could have said that their actions had the blessing of Robert the Bruce, who is supposed to have replied to one asking him what should be done with Soulis after his plot was discovered, 'Boil him if you please, but let me hear no more of him.'

THE WALK: MAP SQUARE:
FROM HERMITAGE   Ordnance Survey Sheet
CASTLE TO THE   79/497960

*Hermitage Castle lies twelve miles south of Hawick on an un-
numbered minor road off the B6399 (Newcastleton) road.
Coming south from Hawick, you drive through Hermitage
village on the B6399, cross Hermitage Water and
immediately turn right on to the minor road where Hermitage
Castle is signposted. There is no public transport service to the
area of the castle.*

*Our walk here follows in the wake of Mary Queen of Scots,
rather than in that of Lord Soulis, for it traces a part of the
ride the Queen made to visit Lord Bothwell at Hermitage
Castle in October 1566.*

*The Queen's biographer, Antonia Fraser, argues that this
famous ride was not scandalous, as Mary's detractors later
made it out to be, but a rational decision taken for reasons of
state. The length of the ride, though considerable, was not
unreasonable and was the kind of riding to which the Queen,
an excellent horsewoman, was well accustomed. Furthermore,
she was accompanied on the ride by her half-brother Moray, a
retinue of courtiers and a number of soldiers – hardly the
attendants of a woman intent on a headlong dash to her lover's
side.*

*Be that as it may, the Queen has provided us with a fine,
not too difficult but slightly adventurous walk, which may
begin at the Castle car park. From here you have two routes to
choose from. You may stick to the road, which follows the
right (west) bank of Hermitage Water north, or you may cross
the bridge into the Castle grounds, turn left past the chapel,
and then follow the river's left bank north.*

*Either way, you will have an attractive walk beside this
picturesque river, tumbling over its stony bed, with its banks
softened by scatterings of trees, and with rolling, grass-
covered hills rising on either side.*

After one and a quarter miles you will come, if you are on the road, to a bridge over Hermitage Water, with a track going north from it towards Old Braidlie. (If you have walked up the left bank of the river, you will join this track at the bridge.)

Four hundred yards or so up the track, a path branches off to the left. This leads you uphill between two small plantations of trees towards the Braidley Burn. The walking here is not difficult, though the presence of other burns draining down off the surrounding hill into Braidley Burn means the land may be boggy. The path follows the left bank of the burn up its valley for three-quarters of a mile, with grassy hills rising on either side – steeply on the western side – to Braidiehope, where two burns coming down the hill on either side of the Queen's Mire meet to become the Braidley Burn.

The path takes you on north, more or less between these two burns, across the slope of the hill to the north of which lies the Queen's Mire. It was here that Mary's horse nearly foundered in the bog, and the Queen lost the enamelled watch which was found two hundred years later and put in the museum at Queen Mary's House in Jedburgh. You will now have walked some three and a quarter miles from Hermitage Castle, much of it over hilly, wet ground, so you may feel that this is a good point at which to turn back. The path carries on north to join up with several other paths and tracks with which this part of the Border country is well endowed.

7. THE RESCUE OF KINMONT WILLIE
Liddesdale

William Armstrong, or Will of Kinmont, came of a notorious clan of Border raiders who at the height of their success in the late sixteenth century could muster, so it was said, up to three thousand horsemen to take part in their sheep-stealing and cattle-rustling raids over the Border into northern England. Their base was Liddesdale in the heart of the Western Marches, whose keeper in the time of Kinmont Willie was Sir Walter Scott of Branxholm, Laird of Buccleuch.

Scott of Branxholm was an ancestor of Sir Walter Scott of poetry and novel fame, which explains how the latter came to include *The Ballad of Kinmont Willie* in his collection of Border ballads; he was naturally interested in the activities of an ancestor of his, though Scott's version of how Kinmont Willie came to be rescued from Carlisle Castle was a highly romanticized version of the facts. This is hardly surprising, for the story of Kinmont Willie is the very stuff from which legends are made.

It was clear, even before they were given an opportunity to kidnap him and bring him to justice, that the lords and landowners on the English side of the Border had had enough of Kinmont Willie. His band of freebooters and reivers had spread havoc and destruction far and wide as they raided valuable flocks of sheep and herds of cattle all along the western end of the Border.

When he had the nerve to turn up, as bold as brass, at a meeting which had been called between the two sides in the perennial Border feud, it was the last straw for the English. The meeting took place on the English side of the

Border in March 1596, and Armstrong accompanied Robert Scott of Haining, who came as Buccleuch's deputy to the meeting. The English were led by Salkeld of Corby, who was the deputy of Lord Scroope, Warden of the English West Marches and based at Carlisle Castle.

Under the law of the time, which was generally scrupulously observed by both sides, a truce was always called on such occasions, and anyone attending a Border meeting knew he would be free from molestation until sunrise on the day after the meeting. The English managed to keep their annoyance hidden during the discussions which took place, but as soon as the Scots had left to return home over the Border, Salkeld decided it was now or never for Kinmont Willie. He had seen Armstrong ride off, so sure of himself that he had only four companions and looking to be in no hurry as they sauntered off, apparently admiring the view of England – and, no doubt, English sheep and cattle – on the way.

Salkeld very quickly gathered together a force of two hundred horsemen and set off over the Border in pursuit of his quarry. He came up with Kinmont Willie on the Scottish side of Liddell Water, still with only four companions, and soon overpowered him. Armstrong, his arms bound behind him, was borne off to England and imprisoned in Carlisle Castle.

Scott of Buccleuch heard the news of Kinmont Willie's kidnapping in his castle stronghold of Branxholm. 'Now Christ's curse on my head,' he shouted, according to Sir Walter Scott, 'But avenged of Lord Scroope I'll be!'

Furious that one of his own representatives should have been taken against the law of truce, Buccleuch appealed to Lord Scroope and to King James on Kinmont Willie's behalf. The weeks passed and neither the English lord nor the Scottish king showed any disposition to do anything for Willie Armstrong, languishing under sentence of death in Carlisle Castle.

Perhaps King James had remembered that his grandfather had felt obliged to hang another Armstrong, Johnnie Armstrong of Gilknockie, and did not feel like disturbing relations with his cousin Elizabeth of England for the sake of a member of the lawless clan. Finally, Buccleuch decided he must take matters into his own hands and avenge the blow to his pride, rescuing Willie Armstrong at the same time.

He began calling out his followers, and by 13 April a force two hundred strong of men from Border clans – Scotts, Armstrongs, Elliots and Graemes – were assembled by the Water of Sark, ten miles from Carlisle, ready to rescue Kinmont Willie. To a casual observer, they would hardly have looked like a serious force, encumbered as they were with scaling ladders, axes, and other tools. But Buccleuch knew what he was about, and led them off at the gallop into England towards Carlisle.

By the time they reached the Castle, the night had turned stormy. It was very dark, and the rain lashed down – all of which greatly assisted the raiding party as they left their horses and began creeping silently round the outer wall of the castle. All was quiet in the castle, and no watchman called out to challenge them.

No doubt it had never occurred to the English that the Scots might send a raiding party to rescue Kinmont Willie from Carlisle, so large and impregnable was it. Even so, Lord Scroope had some difficulty in making his report to Elizabeth's Privy Council seem anything other than a feeble excuse.

To make things sound better, he told the Privy Council that the raiding party had consisted of five hundred men, all armed and appointed with crowbars, scaling ladders, axes and other such objects. But he was quite unable to explain how the mob had gained access to the castle so easily, and fell back on just presenting a bare outline of events.

Buccleuch's men had come 'unto an outerwarde corner of the base courts of this castell, and to the posterne dore of the same', Scroope wrote, nibbling the end of his quill while searching for words that would not sound too inadequate to the Privy Council. 'They undermyned the posterne dore speedily and quietlye and made themselves possessors of the base courte, brake into the chamber where Will of Kinmont was, carried him away . . . and lefte for dead two of the watchmen, hurt a servante of myne, one of Kynmonte's keepers, and were issued againe oute of the posterne before they were descried by the watche of the innerwarde and ere resistance could be made . . .'

Buccleuch had led his men over Eden Water and before galloping home with the rescued Willie,

> He turned him on the other side,
> And at Lord Scroope his glove flung he:—
> 'If ye like na my visit in merry England,
> In fair Scotland come visit me!'

THE WALK:
DINLABYRE TO THE BORDER.

MAP SQUARE:
Ordnance Survey Sheet
79/529922
A 7-mile walk on unpaved forest and fell tracks.

This walk, based on one included in D. G. Moir's well-known Scottish Hill Tracks: Old Highways and Drove Roads (Southern Scotland)*, allows you to discover something of the Armstrong country in Liddesdale and also gives an idea of the sort of territory over which Border raids were run in the generations before the unification of the crowns of Scotland and England.*

Dinlabyre lies near the head of Liddesdale, four and a half miles north-east of Newcastleton on the B6357. This road traces the course of Liddel Water, on the Scottish side of which Kinmont Willie was snatched in the famous – or infamous – English raid. According to D. G. Moir, this road was used from early in the nineteenth century to transport coal over the Border from Northumberland.

The walk begins just to the north of the village, where a forestry track branches east off the B6357. Follow this track south-east and uphill – not very steeply at first but with a steeper gradient after a mile – for about one and a half miles until you reach a point where the track divides. Take the right-hand fork and follow it for just over two miles. You will cross several streams and climb to a height of 1,480 feet on Larriston Fells, with good views of forest and hills all round, before descending to the Border (at 1,287 feet) at a point called Bloody Bush. There is a distance marker here to indicate that you have arrived in England.

Behind you lies the rolling, grassy country of Larriston Fells, with the northern edge of the Newcastleton Forest clothing the western slopes; ahead are the thousands of acres of the Keilder Forest in Northumberland. Parts of both forests come within the area of the Border Forest Park.

8. THE GOOD MAN OF BALLENGEICH
Annandale

The valleys that run south through Dumfries are not called glens, as in the Highlands, but dales, for this is an area that has been anglicized as a result of its long, and not always friendly, contact with the English over the Border. Before the Union of Scotland and England this was a disputed territory and Border raids were a part of everyday life. Today, the peaceful green valleys of Annandale have a pastoral calm, though the brooding presence of castles like Hoddom and Lochmaben indicate a more violent past.

Hoddom Castle.

Near Hoddom is the home of Thomas Carlyle, the eminent Victorian author, which is open to visitors (Good Friday to 31 October daily except Sundays, 10.00–18.00). Carlyle went to school in Annan village where the practice of checking the boundaries is still celebrated in June every year. This ancient custom is also practised at nearby Dumfries, the home of Robert Burns.

The valley of Annandale is the setting for a legend based on the historical facts of the Border raids during the reign of James V of Scotland. James was a man of contrasts. Always anxious to acquire wealth and hoard it, he yet spent a fortune building the beautiful Falkland Palace. Very hard against any, such as the Armstrongs of the Border, who challenged his royal authority, he was yet regarded as a kindly king who took a great interest in his subjects. He often went among his people in the disguise of a poor man, 'the good man of Ballengeich' gaining a reputation as the 'poor man's King'.

During his reign, the Border area around Annandale was in the charge of a certain Sir John Charteris who, although a good Warden of the Marches, performing well his task of keeping the English at bay, was not immune to the temptations to which barons of the day were subject.

It so happened that the son of a rich English Border landowner had been captured and held by the Scots. As was the custom, a ransom was demanded for his return. Sir John Charteris, who conducted the negotiations success-fully, received the money and seeing that it was a sizeable amount, decided to hang on to it. Not long after, the father of the ransomed lad was given an opportunity to get his money back when a young Scot, Wallace Maxwell, was himself captured in a raid. The English kept him close prisoner and demanded a ransom equal to the one they had just paid out. But young Maxwell's family, though once rich, had been impoverished by years of raids from over the Border, and could not raise the money. Unfortunately, Sir John had spent the ransom money and in any case did not feel that the poor young farmer was worth rescuing, even though his father had been George Maxwell, a leader of the Scottish Border forces and a local hero. So he took no immediate notice of the affair.

Wallace Maxwell lived with his widowed mother and was in love with Mary Morrison, a very beautiful girl whom he intended to marry as soon as he had saved up enough money. When young Maxwell was captured and it was known that a ransom was asked for him, his mother and Mary applied for help to Sir John, whose position as Warden of the Marches made him responsible for the safety and welfare of all the people in his part of the Border lands. Sir John refused to see them. Later, having been told of Mary Morrison's great beauty, he agreed to see her.

When Mary appeared at Sir John's headquarters at Amisfield, near Dumfries, and was left alone with him in his private quarters, she soon realized where his real interest lay. Though she loved Maxwell more than any man on earth she was not prepared to pay the price that Sir John was hinting at to obtain his release. Sir John tried everything: reason, cajolery, and even threats, telling her that if he did not pay the ransom – which he was prepared to do in return for one thing – she would never see her lover again. He would die in an English prison. Mary was a strong-minded girl with firm principles, so making her escape from Sir John she set off to seek an audience at Hoddom Castle with King James, whom she knew to be an understanding man, ever ready to listen to his subjects' problems.

King James listened attentively but as he was used to receiving petitions from opportunists and lunatics as well as those really in need, he simply told Mary that he would look into it. Unlike many people in authority who promise to look into things, King James actually did.

In his guise as the good man of Ballengeich, he went to Annandale and set himself outside the cottage of Maxwell, where he pretended to be in distress. The women, seeing the old man bent over his stick, immediately ran to help him, took him into the house and gave him food and drink. The King thanked them and assuring them that he felt better and would be able to continue on his journey, left them and headed in the direction of Sir John's castle. There, he went through the same act but this time no one took any notice of him except the porter who asked him what he wanted at Amisfield. 'I crave an interview with the lord,' said the King. The porter looked surprised at the temerity of an old beggar man, but nevertheless he went away and told Sir John whose reply was that he had no time to talk to the stranger at his gates.

'Tell him,' the King said, 'that I have some important news for him. As I journeyed here I saw the English massing for an attack across the Border.' The porter went off into the depths of the castle again and this time came back with the encouraging reply that his lord would see the old man, but not for at least two hours, for he was at dinner.

'I see,' said the King. 'Well, tell him that he should be lighting the beacons and arousing the countryside or we shall all be dead in two hours.'

The porter looked somewhat alarmed, though the King did not know whether it was at his warning or at the prospect of having to interrupt Sir John once more. At any rate, the porter scuttled off again, nervously wringing his hands. As he disappeared from view, the King threw off his poor man's clothes and summoning a herald who was hiding in the darkness outside the castle gate, ordered him to blow the royal call on his horn. The sound of the horn echoed through the castle courtyards and up the stairs, even penetrating the room in which Sir John was gorging himself at a table laden with food. Dropping a chicken leg that he was about to gnaw the baron leapt to his feet and ran to the balcony. Below him in the courtyard he saw the King and fell on his knees.

'Your Majesty,' he said, 'I had no idea.' Ideas were certainly running around his head, but he could not make head or tail of them. He was filled with alarm, as well he might be, for the reason for the King's visit soon became all too clear. 'You will pay the ransom for young Wallace Maxwell,' the King told Sir John. 'And what is more, you will give him a good farm from your estates or you will not be Warden of the Marches for much longer. You have until next week and I will wait at Hoddom Castle to hear that this has been done.'

Needless to say, everything was done as the King commanded. Thus young Wallace Maxwell got his bride and a farm and everyone except Sir John was happy at the outcome of the affair.

THE WALK:	MAP SQUARE:
A RIVERBANK WALK IN	Ordnance Survey Sheet
THE VICINITY OF	85/153728
HODDOM CASTLE.	An easy afternoon's stroll.

Hoddom Castle, where King James waited to receive Sir John's submission, dates mainly from the fifteenth century and still has a bridged moat, though the present building also has a large nineteenth-century wing to one side. The castle lies two and a half miles south-west of Ecclefechan, birthplace of Thomas Carlyle, on the B725, and three and a half miles north of Annan on the B723.

The grounds of Hoddom Castle contain a large caravan site, but this has not spoiled their attractions, and many local people come here for a pleasant Sunday afternoon walk. The remains of a formally laid-out garden can still be seen in front of the castle, but most of the grounds have informal walks lined with shrubberies. It is all very pretty, and will provide you with an enjoyable afternoon's stroll, with the added interest of a detour to the tower on Repentance Hill, just on the other side of the B725 via a narrow bridge over the road. The path from the castle to the tower is said to have been built by the Lord Herries who built Hoddom Castle, repenting the fact that he had had a church pulled down to make way for his castle.

For a walk along the River Annan, as far as you like, leave the castle grounds by the path which strikes off at an angle of 45 degrees from the moat-and-bridge end of the castle, and takes you down to the river.

THE CENTRAL REGION

9. THE FOUNDING OF HOLYROOD ABBEY
Edinburgh

The Palace of Holyroodhouse, lying at the other end of the Royal Mile from Edinburgh Castle, dates from about 1500 and is still a state palace, being the Queen's official residence in Scotland. It is a major tourist attraction in the city, and thousands of visitors walk through its State Apartments every year, revelling in the history of this ancient building. Many of them fail to take much notice of the ruins of the far more ancient Holyrood Abbey which lies to one side of the Palace's inner quadrangle.

There is, it is true, very little of the original abbey left to be seen – only a Norman arch behind the royal vault can be said to date from the abbey's foundation – but it is enough to recall the legend behind the origin of Holyrood Abbey.

King David I, who ruled Scotland from 1124 to 1153, was the pious son of a pious mother, Queen Margaret, wife of Malcolm III (Canmore). Just as she had built churches and endowed livings in her lifetime, so her son David did too. The great Border Abbeys of Melrose, Jedburgh, Dryburgh and Kelso were all founded in David's reign – if not by him, then under his influence.

Indeed, the King's lavish use of the royal purse for ecclesiastical purposes helped impoverish the Crown, to such an extent that James VI could still complain of his ancestor's improvidence four and a half centuries later.

The abbey at Edinburgh was founded directly by the King as the result, so it is told, of a miraculous happening during the course of a stag hunt.

One day in 1128, the King and few members of his court had ridden out from Edinburgh Castle to hunt deer. The party were spread out among the trees a mile or so from the Castle with the King's hunt servants searching out likely animals and driving them towards the huntsmen. The King was alone in a clearing, when a great stag, enraged at having been disturbed, rushed out from the trees and charged straight at him. It was a very fine animal, with great wide-spreading antlers, which it lowered as it charged.

With no one to help him, and no way of avoiding the animal, the King had to rely on his own strength. As the stag charged, King David side-stepped and grabbed at those terrible antlers, hoping to force the stag's head down and away from him.

As he grasped the antlers, he felt them change shape and substance in his hands. Looking down, he saw that he was holding, not horn antlers, but a wooden cross. The stag disappeared as if it had never been, and the King was left standing with the cross in his hands.

Calling his courtiers to him, the King killed no more deer that day. He returned to Edinburgh Castle, pondering on the significance of his miraculous escape. Surely God, having marked him out for some purpose, had saved him so that he might carry out that purpose.

He retired to bed that night still not understanding the meaning of the miracle. After he had lain asleep some time, he began to dream. He heard a voice, speaking firmly and clearly, telling him that he must found an abbey on the spot where the stag had attacked him.

The next day, the King began drawing up a charter for the foundation of an Augustinian abbey a mile from Edinburgh Castle. The abbey would be called Holy Rood (or Cross), in memory of the King's miraculous escape from death.

In time, David's abbey developed into a royal home, growing from the monks' guest house into a splendid palace, of which the old abbey was the Chapel Royal.

THE WALK:
A WALK IN HOLYROOD
PARK, STARTING AND
FINISHING AT THE
ABBEY.

MAP SQUARE:
Visitors' map, 'Edinburgh:
How Do I Get There',
available from the
Edinburgh Tourist
Information and Accom-
modation Centre,
5 Waverley Bridge.
A 4-mile walk criss-crossing
Holyrood Park, taking in hill
and heath land.

The walk is within the confines of the Park round Holyrood Palace and Abbey. The Palace is open daily throughout the year (Sunday afternoons only in winter) except during royal or state visits.

Most of the Park lies to the south of the Palace, with the Queen's Drive circling its outer edge. Towards the Park's southern boundary, Arthur's Seat (822 feet) rises from the surrounding land to offer from its summit excellent views of Edinburgh and beyond to the sea. Also within the Park, so close to the heart of the city, are three lochs, acres of heath and moorland and the dramatic cliffs of the Salisbury Crags.

The walk is planned to take you as much over grassy and hilly heathland as along metalled roads, so good walking shoes are necessary.

Starting the walk by Holyrood Abbey, you walk south along the path called Croft-on-Righ, past tennis courts, to the Queen's Drive. On the hill opposite here is St Margaret's Well. Once on the Queen's Drive, you follow the road east (i.e. you turn left when you reach the Drive), towards St Margaret's Loch, branching off right after three hundred yards or so up the track to Haggis Knowe and the ruins of St

The Gates of Holyrood House.

Anthony's Chapel, which sits on the hill above St Margaret's Loch.

From here, follow the path which cuts south and east across the Park to rejoin the Queen's Drive at Dunsapie Loch – a walk of about a mile over hilly heathland with Crow Hill on your left hand and Arthur's Seat to your right. (If you want to climb Arthur's Seat, you should branch off the path from St

Anthony's Well, either just south of the well or about half a mile further on.)

From Dunsapie Loch, follow the Queen's Drive back in a westerly direction for another mile and a half until you come to another path branching off the Drive to the right. This path offers you alternative routes back to the abbey. You can take either the path which climbs up quite steeply at first, through Hunters Bog to bring you back down to Haggis Knowe, or you can walk along Radical Road west and north below the line of Salisbury Crags. Each path is about the same distance – a mile and a quarter, and both will bring you to St Margaret's Well and the way back to the abbey.

10.   THE JEALOUS SCULPTOR
Roslin

To the south of Edinburgh in the Pentlands there lies on the North Esk river a small village called Roslin, famous for its fifteenth-century chapel. The wealth of sculpture with which it is decorated makes Roslin Chapel one of Scotland's finest churches.

The chapel was founded in 1446 by William Sinclair, Earl of Orkney and Roslin whose ancestors had come to Britain with William the Conqueror, who according to legend won his lands from Robert the Bruce, wagering his head against the lands that one of his hounds could pull down a deer at a certain burn. He built himself a castle at Roslin and this lies to the west of the chapel on a promontory which extends into the North Esk river. Though destroyed in 1544, the castle was rebuilt as a fortified mansion and these are the ruins you see today. Of the original there are only fragments of passages and dungeons.

As well as Roslin Chapel, Sir William also built a church, so thankful was he to have retained his head! Roslin Chapel became his family's burial place for many generations until 1650; the men of the family were buried in full armour but the tradition was broken by a Sinclair widow who found the custom beggarly and had her dead husband otherwise clothed before his interment.

Although damaged by a mob during the 1688 Revolution, the chapel still contains many beautiful and interesting sculptures including bas-reliefs in the side aisles depicting the Seven Deadly Sins and the Seven Cardinal Virtues. The most important sculpture is the

Prentice Pillar, entwined round which is an exceedingly elaborate carving of leaves, flowers and stems.

At the time when the chapel was built it was necessary to put the work in the charge of a master mason who would carry it out with the help of a band of apprentices. These master masons travelled all over Europe fulfilling the commissions entrusted to them, and the greater their fame the more they were in demand. There was great rivalry between these craftsmen and they were extremely jealous of their reputations.

The master mason hired to work on the chapel at Roslin was no different from other members of his profession and when he received the commission to decorate the chapel he was naturally very pleased and determined to do his best to create a building which would not only honour his patron but do some good to himself as well. To make doubly sure that the quality of his workmanship would be up to the highest standards of the time, the master mason decided to travel to Italy (where were working such masters of his profession as Donatello and Ghiberti, the creator of the great bronze doors of the Florentine Baptistery) to study the latest styles and techniques in sculpture.

Before leaving for Italy, the craftsman left some of the easier jobs – such as the decorative borders round the arches and the foliage on the tops of the columns – for his apprentices to get on with. During the months that he was away, they all busily carried on with their work, chipping away at the stones that had to be fitted together, and carving out the decorative elements under the stern eye of the master mason's chief assistant.

One of the apprentices, who lived with his mother in a cottage overlooking the river, was impatient to be allowed to start carving figures and more interesting subjects than boring foliage. He often stayed on after the others had left at the end of the day's work and carved angels' heads, which he hoped his master would be pleased with when he returned. His mother, who knew something about the jealousy that existed among master masons, tried to dissuade him, telling him that he should wait until his master had returned before doing this work which no apprentice was permitted to touch.

The lad was full of the enthusiasm of youth and, spurred on by his growing mastery of his art, did not heed his mother. As well as the angels' heads he now turned to something much more ambitious – a whole pillar of elaborately carved stones.

When the master mason finally arrived back in Roslin, the boy was eager to show him the work he had done during his absence and at the first opportunity he took him to the corner of the chapel where he had placed the stones that he had carved.

The master mason looked at them, solemnly tapping his stonemason's hammer against the palm of his hand. He had already been told by some of the villagers that the boy had been making some remarkable carvings during his absence and now, seeing how good they were, envy of the boy's talent grew within him. He asked how many people knew about the carvings, and the boy told him frankly that all the people who had visited the chapel had seen them, including the Lord Sinclair who had said that he liked them.

'So,' the master stonemason said, 'you have tried to usurp my place during my absence.'

The apprentice tried to explain that far from wanting to take his place, he was trying to help create the masterpiece which the stonemason himself wanted to build in honour of his master, the Lord Sinclair.

'To honour yourself, you mean,' the stonemason replied and berated the boy for his lack of the proper humility and gratitude appropriate to an apprentice. The boy did not want for spirit, and feeling upset by his master's lack of comprehension, he stood up for himself – which only annoyed his master even more. By now, the words of their argument were echoing round the empty chapel and could be heard even out in the street where a crowd, including the boy's mother, began to gather.

Suddenly, the listening people heard a cry of pain and then silence. They all looked at each other in alarm and foreboding and then the boy's mother led the rush into the chapel where they saw a terrible scene.

The young apprentice lay on the floor with blood oozing from his head. Beside him stood the master stonemason, seemingly transfixed by what he had done. Suddenly becoming aware of the crowd at the door, he gave vent to a cry and ran out of the chapel bellowing like a demented bull.

The apprentice died and the mason was never seen again. The Prentice's Pillar was assembled and put in a place of honour at the end of the south aisle. Another of the sculptors working on the chapel made a carving of three heads – the apprentice boy, his grieving mother, and the master mason – and this was added to the carvings at the end of the nave. Thus the apprentice boy and his jealous master were immortalized in stone.

THE WALK: MAP SQUARE:
A SHORT WALK,   Ordnance Survey Sheet
FOLLOWING ROADS AND   66/267648
PATHS TO ROSLIN CHAPEL. A 1½-mile walk from
                                         Bilston to Roslin.

Roslin lies off the A701 road to Edinburgh between the Pentland and the Moorfoot Hills. Green woods border the valley of the North Esk river on which the village stands. Opposite the village, on the east side of the river, is Wallace's

Roslin Chapel.

Cave in which the Scots hero hid during one of his many battles against the English, while further north is Hawthornden Castle on the site of the house of the poet William Drummond of Hawthornden.

If you are coming from Edinburgh to this pleasant part of Midlothian, you can have an enjoyable walk in the area of Roslin by leaving your car at Bilston (where a bus service from Edinburgh also stops). There is a path from the centre of this small village past Dryden Tower and across the land of Langhill Farm to Dryden Mains, and so to a minor road, about three-quarters of a mile from Bilston. Turn right here and, following the line of the dismantled railway walk into Roslin. The chapel is by the river on the east side of the village and is open weekdays from Easter to October. It is still a functioning church so is open only for worship on Sundays.

The castle stands on a promontory over the river and visitors are not encouraged, but you can get a good idea of its size and extent from the outside. If you have a real interest in seeing more of it, you should apply to the caretaker.

As the walk from Bilston to Roslin is only one and a half miles, you may want to extend it by crossing the North Esk by the footbridge at Roslin and following the river bank round Roslin and north to Hawthornden and Polton, a very lovely riverside walk of about a mile.

11. ROBERT THE BRUCE AND THE SPIDER
Bannockburn

The battlefield where Robert Bruce routed an English army in June 1314 is today the property of the National Trust for Scotland. Its 58 acres lie two miles south of Stirling, whose impressive castle perched on a crag reminds one that this was a strategic strongpoint guarding the doorway to the north and was once occupied by the English when Edward I was trying to assert his claim to be feudal lord of Scotland. Bannockburn itself lies just off the M80 on the stream that gives it its name.

According to legend, the victory at Bannockburn was inspired by a spider. Bruce had made himself King of Scotland in place of the Balliol line and without much support from the Scots, after the defeat and death of William Wallace in 1305. Bruce had been defeated in his first encounters with the English, and with his army gone, many of his friends hanged and he himself outlawed, seemed to have little hope of becoming King in Scotland permanently. He was a hunted man and Edward I of England, the 'Hammer of the Scots', was determined to wipe out any trace of the resistance that Wallace and Bruce had tried to offer to domination by the English.

Edward's merciless campaign helped to inspire in the Scots a hatred of the English and a determination to drive them back beyond the Border. But they needed a leader.

It was while hiding in a cave that Bruce is reputed to have been encouraged to persevere in the face of seemingly impossible odds. The location of this famous cave is variously ascribed to the Isle of Arran, to the island of Rathlin off the Mull of Kintyre, and the Kirkpatrick

Fleming near to the Border at Gretna Green, where an inscription confirms the claim in the rock of a local cave.

Robert the Bruce, the legend tells us, lay in the cave one night wondering whether he had better not give up his dream of freeing Scotland of the English. True, Edward I – the 'Hammer' – was now dead and his son, Edward II, seemed a much weaker figure. But the English forces were still strong. Thus Bruce pondered. Then he noticed a spider.

The creature was dropping from an outcrop of rock and attempting to swing itself to another projecting ledge in order to establish a line on which it could start to build its web. Bruce watched as the spider swung down towards its target and saw it miss and remain dangling out of reach.

After a moment, the spider wound up its silken line again and returned to the starting point. A second time, the spider spun out its fine thread and swung towards the projection. Again it missed. Once more it had to rewind its line and return to its vantage point.

Having nothing else to do, Bruce studied the spider and its predicament. There was no doubt that the point that the spider was aiming at was the only one that would provide the appropriate anchorage for its web, but there was equally little doubt that its chances of success were slim. For an hour and then another hour, Bruce watched the determined efforts of the little creature and as he did so he felt inspired by its courage and perseverance.

When at last the spider managed to attach its thread to the spot that it had been aiming at, Bruce knew what he must do. Leaving his hiding place the following day, he began to collect another army together and in a short while was waging a guerilla war against the English who were unable to return his blows effectively, because they were laden down with horses and equipment and so could not move fast.

On 23 June 1314 Bruce found himself facing the strongest force that the English had ever assembled. The English army, which had come north in such strength to raise the siege of Stirling Castle by Robert Bruce's brother Edward, was led by its King, Edward II, in person.

Between the two armies lay the burn of Bannock and to the west was the gorge through which the burn rushed headlong as it flowed into the flatter, marshy ground where the armies faced each other.

At the first encounter, the English crossed the stream but so well had Robert Bruce prepared his ground, they were unable to make any headway before night fell.

Perhaps during that night Bruce remembered again the lesson of the spider for next day he made a determined onslaught upon the much larger force of the enemy and, disregarding his previous failures when up against English forces, he completely overwhelmed his foe. The English army was routed, and Edward II fled the battlefield. Some say he did not stop galloping until he reached Dunbar.

Scotland was at last on the road to acknowledgement of her independence thanks to Bruce's determination in the face of impossible odds.

THE WALK:
A WALK ROUND
STIRLING OLD TOWN,
BEGINNING AND ENDING
AT THE TOURIST
INFORMATION OFFICE.

MAP SQUARE:
The Stirling Old Town Walk, a leaflet prepared by the Stirling Tourist Association and available from the Tourist Information Office, Dumbarton Road, Stirling. A 1¼-mile walk taking in many of the interesting buildings and sites in the historic part of Stirling.

The site of the battle of Bannockburn does not provide much interesting walking, as most of it is built over. The area around the National Trust for Scotland's Bannockburn site, 58 acres round the Borestone which is traditionally the site of Bruce's headquarters before the battle, is also not very exciting walking country. It is flat field and farm land and, although the panorama views from the Rotunda are very good, once again opportunities for an interesting walk are slight.

For our Bannockburn walk, therefore, we are retreating, like Edward II after the battle, to Stirling Castle.

A castle has stood on Stirling Rock for eight hundred years, and today's castle is the magnificent point of this one-and-a-quarter mile walk round Stirling. The walk begins at Dumbarton Road, near the Tourist Information Office, which is well signposted on the road into town from Bannockburn, so you should find it without difficulty. There is a car park nearby.

From Dumbarton Road, you walk along the Back Walk, partway up which is the Watchtower and the 'hangman's entry' through the old town wall. You then walk beside the Town Wall, passing such places of interest as the Erskine Marykirk, the three-storey Victorian prison, and the Guildhall, which was originally built as a hospice for poor Guild members. Bearing right at the top of the Town Wall, you pass the Holy Rude Church, Stirling's principal church for five hundred years.

Turning right again into St John Street, you are now into a part of Stirling whose layout has not changed very much since the twelfth century. The seventeenth-century houses immediately on your right stand on the site of the medieval livestock, or 'fleshers', market.

Walk down the left-hand side of St John Street, turning left at the first corner. On the opposite corner (Spittal Street) stands Robert Spittal's house, a fine example of seventeenth-century domestic architecture. The next turning left brings

81

you into Broad Street, with the Murcat Cross (only the unicorn on top is original: the rest was reconstructed in 1891) in the centre and more seventeenth-century houses on the opposite side of the street.

From Broad Street, you turn along Castle Wynd, pausing to look at Mars Wark, the remains of a Renaissance mansion built by the Earl of Mar, Regent of Scotland in 1572, which stands on the left-hand side.

You are now approaching the Esplanade and the way into Stirling Castle. Look out for the Landmark Visitor Centre to one side of the Esplanade. This is a good point from which to view the surrounding countryside. There is an audio-visual theatre here giving a good account of Stirling's history and an exhibition of Stirling life in the nineteenth century.

You may want to miss the interior of the castle on this walk, making it the object of a separate visit. If you do decide to visit it as part of your walk, you should allow yourself two or three hours at least, just to get an idea of what lies behind the castle walls. You will find a fine palace, built in the Renaissance style of the fifteenth and sixteenth centuries, a chapel, a royal mint, a military museum, and many other places of interest.

From the castle, the walk takes you down from the Esplanade via a flight of steps to the small Valley Cemetery, which lies between the castle and the Church of the Holy Rude. Crossing the Valley Cemetery, with the King's Garden on your right, you reach the Town Walk again and the way back to your starting point in Dumbarton.

12. THE FREEZING OF LOCH KATRINE
The Trossachs

Loch Katrine is the largest of the three lochs which, joined by small rivers, provide a dominant element in the glorious scenery of mountain, moorland and wooded glen which make up the Trossachs ('the bristly country', as its name means). This small stretch of country in western Perthshire, only five miles wide, and lying round the southern end of Loch Katrine, packs into its area so much beauty and variety of scenery, that it is often described as 'the Highlands in miniature'. It might also be called 'Glasgow's back garden', for it lies relatively close to the great city and on summer weekends is usually dense with cars, picnickers, campers and holiday coaches.

Loch Katrine has a curved shape, with many promontories, so it is impossible to see all of its ten-mile length from any one point. This helps explain the popularity of the fine old Victorian steamer, the *Sir Walter Scott*, which takes visitors on sight-seeing trips up the loch to Stronachlachar.

The trippers will have pointed out to them in the loch Ellen's Isle, named after Ellen Douglas, heroine of Scott's 'The Lady of the Lake', a poem which achieved such fame that it brought tourists flocking to the Trossachs in their thousands in the early nineteenth century – as they still do. Present-day tourists are looking at a rather larger and deeper loch than Sir Walter Scott's admirers knew, for Loch Katrine became one of the main sources of Glasgow's water in 1859, and its water level was raised by nearly twenty feet.

Because it is so deep, and also has a fairly strong current

Loch Katrine.

owing to the fact that it flows into the Teith, a tributary of the Forth, Loch Katrine never freezes over. Our story, current in the folklore of the area, tells of the one time the loch did freeze.

It was a week or so before Christmas, one year many generations ago, and young, charming and friendly George Macduff had just persuaded beautiful Kate from Stronachlachar to marry him. In truth, Kate, despite her aunt's misgivings, had needed little persuasion for George was indeed a very attractive young man, liked by everyone around Loch Katrine.

Until he had clapped eyes on Kate, George had had no thought of marriage, for his life was very good as it was. He had a piece of land, on the stretch of loch shore opposite Stronachlachar, where he could hunt and trap all the meat he needed. His cottage was warm and snug, with a patch of vegetables growing nearby, and his boat, which he kept moored to the shore by his cottage, enabled him to catch all the fish he wanted. He also used it to row over to Stronachlachar to see his friends and perhaps play at a wedding or celebration, for he was an excellent piper, much in demand for his playing.

It was at one such gathering that George had seen Kate for the first time, her pretty face flushed pink with happiness as she danced a reel to George's piping. There and then, George decided that bachelor freedom was not enough; he wanted a wife, and Kate was his choice.

When they became betrothed, Kate, a devout and pious girl, gave George a medallion of St Catherine, her patron saint and Loch Katrine's, as a token of her love. George, rather extravagantly, said that only death would part him from it, but Kate's aunt was not impressed. She knew George to be a godless young man, who had never set foot inside the church in his life and who, if he ever mentioned God and His saints, did so with no respect at all.

The aunt liked George, but she could not rid herself of the suspicion that he was interested in Kate, who was her dead father's heiress, as much for her money as for her beauty. She suggested that Kate should test George's devotion by asking him to accompany her to the Christmas Eve service in the church at Stronachlachar, taking part in every aspect of it.

Kate did ask George, and at first he demurred. He would be happy to escort her to church, but could he not just wait outside for her? Kate looked so unhappy at this, that George capitulated and agreed to go to church with her.

Having thus decided, George was going to do it in style. He went home and sat down to polish his dirk and his plaid brooch, and to put a new feather in his bonnet. He was cleaning his boots when there was a knock on the door, and a tall, handsome and decidedly suave-looking man walked in. His black beard was elegantly trimmed, and George noticed one point in particular – his boots were clean of snow, though it was snowing heavily outside.

As the laws of hospitality required, George offered his visitor a seat by the fire and a dram of whisky, both of which were accepted. Then the visitor came straight to the point: he was the Devil, and had come to save one whom he had always considered his own from the clutches of the God-fearing. He did not care to see his satanic cause betrayed, and he hoped George would consider well before going to church with Kate.

George replied, equally reasonably, that he had promised Kate and that he did not wish to hurt her, or make her cry. The Devil pooh-poohed these misgivings. Kate would not mind, especially if George were to offer her the jewels the Devil intended giving him, along with the means to catch more fish or trap more game than George had every done in his life.

George wavered . . . but a promise was a promise. The Devil said George should repudiate it, as a sign of his respect for his devilish visitor. Then he stood up and left as abruptly as he had come.

George pondered for a long time, but eventually the thought of Kate's smile and the light in her eyes won out over the Devil's tempting offer, and the young man jumped to his feet, put on his bonnet and cloak, and went out into the cold night to his boat.

It was gone. Someone had loosened the mooring, and it had floated away. George looked in despair at the lights of Stronachlachar shining across the water. The church bells were already ringing, and he would never be able to walk round the loch in time to take Kate to church. He took out Kate's token and looked at St Catherine's image. His fingers clenched round the medallion, then he returned it to his pocket.

As he did so, he saw an extraordinary thing happen to the waters of Loch Katrine. A thick sheet of ice was spreading out over the surface of the water. Wider and wider it grew, until the ice had reached George's feet where he stood on the shore.

Stepping gingerly at first, then running as if his life depended on it, George crossed Loch Katrine to where Kate was waiting for him. He ignored the cry of fury and the string of curses which exploded behind him, took Kate's arm, and walked into church.

As he and Kate knelt to pray for their future together, the ice of Loch Katrine cracked and split and melted away.

THE WALK:	MAP SQUARE:
A WALK ALONG THE SHORE OF LOCH KATRINE AT STRONACHLACHAR.	Ordnance Survey Sheet 56/401101 Walk as far as you wish.

The nearest large town to Loch Katrine is Callander, a gateway to the Highlands which lies on the A84 north of Stirling. West of the town, the A821 skirts the north shores of Loch Venacher and Loch Achray before bending south to Aberfoyle. A minor road leads off from this bend to finish at the large car and coach park at the southern end of Loch Katrine. To reach Stronachlachar, on the southern shore of the loch two miles from its head, you must follow the A821 down towards Aberfoyle and branch off on to the B829 just before the centre of the village. This road, which is signposted Stronachlachar and Inversnaid, is a very pretty, tree-lined route which passes two small lochs before meeting Loch Katrine again. It is also hilly, single track, and often crowded in summer, so the going is slow.

Stronachlachar is basically the calling point and pier for lake steamers, though there are a few houses as well. It is in the care of the Strathclyde Water Authority and is very neat indeed. The hedges are clipped, the gravel in the car park raked, the pier, rails and buildings which house the public lavatories sparkling with paint.

The water authority has constructed a private road round the northern end of Loch Katrine, which walkers and cyclists, but not car drivers, may use. You will find the road just beyond the houses set among trees to the north of the car park and pier head.

The country round this end of Loch Katrine is in marked contrast to the wooded and more gentle beauty of that of the Trossachs to the south-east. Here, the land is bleak and barren, but has its own special beauty. Round the head of the loch, on its north shore, the way is heavily strewn with boulders.

You could follow this road all the way round the north shore of the loch to the pier head and its foot, but we think that a *shorter walk of a mile or two, before turning back to Stronachlachar, is probably sufficient to give you the feel of the land.*

13. THE BOGLES OF THE HOWFF
Dundee

Dundee is a fine city on the Firth of Tay and is the fourth largest in Scotland in terms of population. The centre of the town lies along Nethergate and High Street, off City Square. Among the landmarks are St Mary's Tower, known as the Old Steeple, which was built in the fifteenth century. It dominates the City Churches, four churches built round the Tower. The more recent architecture of Caird Hall rises impressively over City Square. High Street curves round into Commercial Street which leads to the Albert Institute, a Gilbert Scott gothic-style building housing a library, art gallery and museum. A few steps along Meadowside, which runs past the Museum, is an old burial ground called The Howff which was Dundee's main burial place for three hundred years, as well as being a meeting place (howff).

Long before it was closed, the cemetery started to become very crowded with the dead and their ghosts, so much so that the ghosts, or bogles, began to move into the houses bordering it. For some reason that has not been recorded, the bogles' favourite house was one that belonged to the local doctor. Though the doctor did not take much notice of the bogles that first arrived, he began to take exception to them when their numbers increased and their behaviour worsened.

Little by little, his house became a bedlam with a continuous cacophony of groans and shrieks and a constant movement of his furniture and possessions. Though he remonstrated with the bogles, they took no notice of the good doctor and in the end he decided to shut the house up and move to Edinburgh for a while, hoping that the bogles, finding their adopted home cold and untenanted, would move elsewhere to a warmer and cosier abode.

While in Edinburgh, the doctor forgot about the bad behaviour of the bogles and almost persuaded himself that he had imagined the whole thing. Eventually, he went back to Dundee but no sooner was he home than his troubles began anew. He could hardly leave his practice again, so the doctor carried on even though he seldom got a good night's sleep and was becoming thoroughly exhausted with the nervous strain of having to put up with the bogles. His haggard appearance was noticed by his friends, who were becoming very anxious about him but could not suggest a remedy for the tiresome state of affairs.

One day, the doctor of Dundee was taking a dram of whisky with a doctor of philosophy, and began telling him about the bogles. It was almost the only subject he ever talked about now, for the bogles had become an obsession. His friend nodded sympathetically and then gave it as his opinion that it was simply all in the doctor's mind and that the answer to his problem was to find a young girl who did not believe in bogles and invite her to live in the house with him.

The doctor was not very convinced by his friend's plan but decided that anything was worth trying to get rid of the pests, so he started asking around among his patients and friends until, finally, one of them told him about a girl from Blairgowrie who had not a shadow of doubt that bogles did not exist. The doctor went to Blairgowrie and using all his powers of persuasion, managed to get the girl to return to Dundee with him.

No sooner were they in the house than the girl became

very busy, cleaning the place up and letting in more light and air than the house had seen in many a day. The doctor could still hear the bogles rattling around the house but their noises seemed to become weaker as the house became brighter.

'Do you not hear them?' the doctor enquired, but the young girl did not even hear him for she was busy shaking out carpets and emptying drawers of the accumulated rubbish of years.

One day as the doctor entered the house after a visit to one of his patients, it suddenly came to him that the place he now resided in bore little resemblance to the one in which he had lived for most of his adult life. All the walls were freshly done in brightly patterned papers and the carpets were as colourful as the meadows in springtime. Moreover, all the woodwork of the floors, bannisters and furniture gleamed with polish and the brass looked like burnished gold. But what struck him most was that the house was now so silent that he could even hear himself breathing.

All this transformation had been brought about by the girl from Blairgowrie who did not believe in bogles and suddenly the doctor knew that he could not contemplate a life without her. As he stood in the hall removing his coat he was seized with a fear that she had gone, for there was no sound in the house. He rushed into the living room, but she was not there, then into the dining room, but she was not there either.

When he found her in the kitchen busily cleaning the silver she seemed not at all surprised at his proposal of marriage and as she accepted she smiled a secret smile. And as for the bogles, they admitted defeat and kept out of the doctor's house ever after.

A CITY WALK IN THE · City walk map available
ANCIENT ROYAL BURGH · from Tourist Information
OF DUNDEE, BEGINNING · Office, City Square.
AT THE HOWFF. · A stroll in the city.

The approach to Dundee over the Tay Bridge offers an instant
panoramic view of the city which has been a royal burgh for
over eight hundred years. The first impression is of a port and
industrial community, with an army of high-rise blocks rising
on the eastern skyline of the volcanic hill on which the city is
built, but there is plenty to see in the way of historical
monuments once you are in the town.

The centre of these is the Howff, originally a meeting place
of the guilds where lively negotiations took place. After Mary
Queen of Scots presented it to the city as a burial place, it

Dundee.

became a gathering point for those who were past earthly communion. The cemetery, with its neat gravestones, interesting tombs and silent trees, strikes a solemn but not disagreeable note amid the cacophony of Dundee's busy thoroughfares. As a starting point for a city walk it is ideal.

Begin by going east along Meadowside; in front of you is the Library, Museum and Art Galleries building, a nineteenth-century gothic-style structure. Turning behind this you come to Panmure Street which leads into King Street and Cowgate. Here is the only remaining gateway of the old city wall which was demolished after the rising of 1745. Retrace your steps and turn left to Seagate where you turn right and head for St Paul's Episcopal Cathedral. In front of it is Castle Hill, its name and a plaque being the only remaining evidence of the existence of a castle here. You now enter the busy High Street lined with shops and stores; to your left appears the large open space of City Square. Here is Caird Hall, the city hall and council chambers, with its extensive colonnaded front, and the site of the town house of the Lairds of Strathmartine.

Rejoining the High Street, turn left and when you enter Nethergate you will see the tower of the City Churches. The famous old steeple is all that remains of the church that was built in the fifteenth century. A garrison in the old Steeple served to protect the town's inhabitants during the Cromwellian invasion by General Monk. In the pleasant gardens surrounding the steeple is the Mercat Cross, a replica of the original which stood at Seagate.

From the Old Steeple you can return to the Howff along Willison Street to complete your town stroll.

For a longer walk you will have to go out of the city via Marketgate and Lochee Road to Dudhope Park at the top of the hill. Dudhope Park's 22 acres are all that remain of the grounds of Dudhope Castle which still stands beside the Lochee Road. The castle was built by the Constables of Dundee among whom was John Graham of Claverhouse, 'Bonnie Dundee', who was born at Old Claverhouse Castle, to the north-east of the city.

An even larger park is Camperdown, 735 acres in extent. Apart from a zoo, riding school and the golf museum in Camperdown House, there are extensive paths through woods and over hill and dale for walkers of all grades of experience.

THE GRAMPIANS AND NORTH-EAST

The Satanic Lover

The Eleven Brothers

The Loch Con Murder

The Ghost of Killiecrankie

The Monster of the Dee

The Witch of Mar

The Burial at Carrbridge

The Battle of Culloden

The Ghost of Rait Castle

14. THE SATANIC LOVER
Dunkeld

When you are approaching Dunkeld on the A9 from Perth you will first of all come to Birnam and its wood, whose appearance at the Castle of Dunsinane spelt doom for Macbeth. Dunkeld spreads across the River Tay in a steep wooded valley and is a most delightful little cathedral town with a long history. It was once the Pictish capital and later

Dunkeld.

the centre of Christian Scotland after the monks of Iona had been driven away from their island by the Norsemen.

The most important building in Dunkeld is undoubtedly its cathedral which dates from the ninth century. Most of the cathedral is now a ruin; it suffered when Dunkeld was burnt by covenanters to prevent the taking of the town by the victorious Highlanders after the Battle of Killiecrankie. The fourteenth-century choir has been restored and is the parish church. Other old houses dating from just after Killiecrankie may be found, beautifully restored, in Cathedral Street, Old Dunkeld.

Many years ago, there lived in one of these houses along Cathedral Street a young girl whose natural innocence was still unspoiled by the wicked ways of the world. This maid worked at the Manse and during her leisure hours liked nothing better than to stroll into the wooded hills and watch the birds at play and the wild flowers growing under the trees. It was during one of these walks that she met a man who was so good-looking and spoke to her so courteously and gently that she, innocent as she was, immediately fell in love with him.

She told no one of this encounter, but every time she went into the woods after that she found the courteous stranger waiting for her. Being a shy girl, she gave no indication of her feelings for him, but these were growing stronger every time they met.

He seemed equally attracted to her. Eventually, one day he said simply and sincerely that since he had met her, he had had only one thought in his mind which was that he should marry her.

This put the girl into such an emotional turmoil that she ran away back down to Dunkeld without stopping to bid the stranger goodbye. As she hurried breathlessly down Cathedral Street, she collided with the Minister. He, having always thought of the maid as a quiet, well-behaved

100

lass, was now astonished to see her in such a state of disarray and excitement. Being a man of the world, he showed no surprise but took the girl by the arm and calmed her down. It was not long before he had drawn from her the reason for her unusual emotional state.

When he had heard her story, the Minister felt grave misgivings about the whole thing but, again, he was sensible enough not to show his feelings. Instead, he suggested gently to the girl that she should invite her friend down to the Manse so that he, the Minister, could have the pleasure of his acquaintance. The girl accepted the invitation happily: she wanted to show off her lover and – perhaps – boast, just a little, of her conquest.

A few days later, the girl brought her friend down to the Manse. Despite his suspicions, the Minister had to agree that it was seldom that one came across such a pleasant fellow as the young man who was taking tea with him. Towards the end of the visit, however, the Minister saw something that gave him a dismaying shock. From under the cloak that the stranger had kept wrapped around him throughout the visit, the Minister saw the tip of one of his feet. It looked more like a cloven hoof than a shoe. At first, the Minister could hardly believe his eyes, but later, having had another opportunity to examine the protruding shoe more closely, he was sure that it had a pronounced cleavage down its centre.

When the stranger had gone, the Minister, not wishing to alarm the girl but determined to bring the hooves to her attention, began to comment on the stranger's pleasant appearance and manners, and on his rather unusual feet.

Finding a sympathetic confidant, the girl poured out her feelings to the Minister, agreeing with everything he said except his description of her lover's feet which she said were not unusual but only shod in the most beautiful pair of black shoes that she had ever seen.

Realizing that love is blind, the Minister did not press the point, but when the girl announced that she was going to accept the stranger as her husband and wanted the Minister to perform the marriage ceremony, the priest became thoroughly alarmed. He knew it was hopeless to try and persuade the besotted young girl that the man on whom she was lavishing her innocent affections was none other than Satan himself. After all, even someone much more aware of the ways of the world would doubt anything so unlikely. He also acknowledged that to oppose her might simply have the effect of driving her into the Devil's arms. He therefore pretended to agree and even set the date for the wedding.

When the day arrived, the Minister had already made his plans for outwitting the evil stranger. Standing before the congregation, he announced that he would perform the ceremony but, since marriage was a serious step, he wanted to allow time for reflection before uttering the final and irrevocable words of the service. He would therefore use the procedure customary at local auctions before a final offer was accepted. This consisted of placing a candle horizontally on a holder and lighting it simultaneously at both ends; when the fire had reached the middle and the candle was consumed this sealed an agreement. Thus, in the case of the marriage, the bride would not be the stranger's wife until the candle had burnt itself out.

The Minister could see that the stranger was not very happy about this unorthodox method of conducting the ceremony, but since there were others present and he did not want to cause a bad impression among those who might be his future clients he said nothing and just nodded his agreement.

The candle burned slowly from each end towards the middle while the Minister made a long and tedious sermon about matrimony and its obligations, and the Devil tapped his hoof irritably on the floor. The girl was lost in a romantic dream and hardly noticed what was going on. The congregation looked curiously at the stranger in his dark cloak and wondered where he had come from, who his relatives were and why he had picked on the young girl from the Manse. Their curiosity seemed almost tangible in the small enclosed chapel and it made the Devil uneasy. He contained himself, however, calming his anxiety with the thought that in a short while the young and innocent girl would be in his power.

The candle burnt away at both ends, shortening to three inches, then to two, then one, as the wax gathered in a pool under it. It was hardly more than half an inch long when the Minister suddenly stopped his sermon and, with an abrupt 'Well, there we are now', picked up the candle and swallowed it whole, muttering as he looked at the Devil, 'That's one marriage that will never be consummated then.'

Realizing that he had been tricked, the Devil's face grew black with fury. Then, with a terrible cry, he launched himself into the air and shot out through the church roof, leaving a trail of sulphurous smoke that set the congregation coughing and spluttering as they recovered from their astonishment.

As for the young girl, it was a terrible shock to her to learn that devils can masquerade as men, but it lessened the later shocks of discovering that men can also be devils.

THE WALKS:	MAP SQUARE:
1. FROM BIRNAM VILLAGE TO THE TOP OF BIRNAM HILL.	1. Ordnance Survey Sheet 52/031416
2. FROM DUNKELD TO THE LOCH OF LOWES NATURE RESERVE.	2. Ordnance Survey Sheet 52/027426

Two relatively short walks to give you a good introduction to the beauties of Dunkeld.

Dunkeld and Birnam lie on either side of the River Tay in a beautiful wooded valley fifteen miles north of Perth. A fine bridge by Thomas Telford takes the main road, the A9(T), from Perth over the Tay, and the ruins of Dunkeld Cathedral stand in a lovely tree-lined setting on the banks of the river. There are many attractive walks and trails to be discovered in the forests here, for some of which pamphlets may be obtained in the NTS information centre near the cathedral.

Our FIRST SUGGESTED WALK here is quite short and, though it is uphill, it is not very steep. Start the walk by the Dunkeld and Birnam railway station, which lies at the end of a short road south of the A9 in Birnam. At the north end of the station is a lane from which you will find a path ascending Birnam Hill (1,324 feet).

The walk to the summit is pleasantly wooded, is less than two miles, and not too strenuous. The view is well worth the effort. Below, you can see the streets of Dunkeld and the cathedral, with the Rock of Dunkeld, Craigia-Barns, appearing through its covering of trees beyond. The north-western panorama takes in Schiehallion beyond Loch Tummel and Ben More further south by Loch Lomond. Admirers of Shakespeare's Macbeth *may be interested to pick out Dunsinane, about twelve miles to the south-east, where the Thane of Cawdor saw his doom moving towards him in the shape of Birnam Wood, thus fulfilling a prophecy.*

*The SECOND SUGGESTED WALK in the Dunkeld area
is included as a reminder that among the forest walks and trails
in which the area abounds, there is also one to a lochside nature
reserve. This is the Loch of Lowes Nature Reserve, belonging
to the Scottish Wildlife Trust, where the birds and animals
given protection include ospreys. A hide has been built
especially to allow visitors a view of the rare and beautiful
birds. There is also a Visitor Centre with good displays
explaining the ecology of the area.*

*To reach the Loch of Lowes Nature Reserve, which lies two
miles from Dunkeld, walk north up the A9 through Dunkeld
town, turning right on to a track to Spoutwells, north of the
golf course. This brings you out on to the A923, where you
turn right and follow the road for rather less than half a mile
to a minor road going off to the right to Lowes and
Catchpenny. Follow this road around the south-western end of
Loch of Lowes to the nature reserve one and a quarter miles
from the turning.*

15. THE ELEVEN BROTHERS
Glen Errochty

Glen Errochty runs from Struan to Trinafour with Loch Errochty a mile further to the west. A minor road off the B847 reaches the loch, the B847 itself turning south at the village and heading down to Kinloch Rannoch. Glen Errochty is a steep-sided valley. Its northern slopes are bare, but a thick covering of forest, the Tummel Forest which stretches over the hill to Loch Tummel, covers the southern slopes. In the centre of the forest, at its highest point – which is Meall Reamhar (1,603 feet) – the land is clear of trees and there are fine views in all directions. To the north-west of Meall Reamhar lies another open space – the Creag of Tulloch, and further west still is Cragan Liath Mor. A track leads up the hill to Cragan Liath Mor from Errochty Water which is crossed by a bridge leading to the B847. A short distance to the west of the bridge there was once a farm where the Laird of Muirlaggan lived with his eleven sons.

Ten of the Laird's sons were strong, active boys who enjoyed the open-air life and spent much of their time hunting, fishing and roaming over the hills. The eleventh son was a slender pale-faced boy who lacked the robustness of his brothers and was, in consequence, a constant butt of their jokes. When the other young men went hunting this youngest son would walk along Errochty Water or roam about the woods lost in his private dreams.

One morning, when the deer-stalking season had just begun, the brothers decided to go into the Tummel Forest armed for the chase. With them went their stag hounds and, on this occasion, their youngest brother.

Tummel Forest.

All morning they stalked the elusive deer, but without success. As midday approached they found themselves on the summit called Cragan Liath Mor, 'The Big Grey Rock'. Here they sat down and opened the bag of provisions they had brought with them and took a drink out of the flagon of whisky that they had taken it in turns to carry.

As they ate, they threw bits of their food at the two stag hounds who snatched at them hungrily, the quicker one grabbing the morsel first. It happened that one piece of food landed exactly between the two hounds who, rushing at it, collided in mid-leap. This set them snarling and snapping at each other and before they could be stopped there was a full-blooded fight going on.

The brothers, who were a wild and pugnacious lot, egged the dogs on, each urging on the hound that was his particular favourite. Only the youngest brother refrained from joining in for he was as much upset by the savagery of the dogs as by the brutish behaviour of his brothers.

As the fight went one way and then the other, with both dogs bleeding but refusing to give in, the opposing factions among the brothers began a verbal aggression which soon turned to fisticuffs and then to an all-out brawl with stones and sticks and hunting knives.

Young Muirlaggan looked on with horror at the senseless and brutal spectacle, his mind aghast at the thought that these men who were viciously trying to kill each other were his own kin.

He watched one of them crushing another's head with a rock while a third staggered down the slope with a wound in his throat from which the blood pumped like a red fountain. He wanted to cry out but no sound came. As if in a terrible nightmare, he saw his brothers dying before his eyes until at last only two remained and these, both bloodied and mortally wounded, fell to the ground and, rolling towards him, died at his feet as he leaped up in horror.

With a terrible shriek of pain young Muirlaggan ran down the hill, his eyes blinded with tears. Arriving at the farm he told his father the appalling story of how the deer-stalking party had ended. The old man would not believe him and together they climbed the hill again so that the Laird of once-peaceful Muirlaggan could see the massacre of his family for himself.

All afternoon the Laird and his son toiled to make cairns for their dead and as the sun set they went slowly down the hill. The blow was too much for the old man who died soon after. So, out of the fine family of Glen Errochty, only the peace-loving youngest son remained. His life, too, was blighted because he was haunted for the rest of his days by the scene he had witnessed at Cragan Liath Mor.

THE WALK:
FROM THE B847 IN GLEN ERROCHTY, TWO AND A HALF MILES EAST OF TRINAFOUR, UP CRAGAN LIATH MOR IN THE TUMMEL FOREST.

MAP SQUARE:
Ordnance Survey Sheet 42/767637
A walk – maximum length just over 6 miles – in the northern part of the Tummel Forest where the eleven brothers went hunting. Not too strenuous, but the path is rough.

Errochty Water flows down the attractive Glen Errochty, edged with the conifers of the Tummel Forest to the south, and with hills and grass-covered farmland to the north.

Blairfettie, where once lived the sons of the Laird of Muirlaggan, is still a pleasant-looking farm which you will pass one and a half miles out of Trinafour on the B847 as it follows the course of Errochty Water to Calvine.

Passing Blairfettie, you drive for just over a mile to where a milestone on the left-hand side of the road will alert you to a right turn immediately opposite. Follow this track a few yards across a wooden, unrailed bridge over the river and a cattle grid to a T-junction. The left-hand arm goes to Bochonie. The right-hand arm, which has a chain across it to stop vehicles entering, is a rough and rutted track which curves round into the forest. Here the walk begins.

The way ahead of you will take you through coniferous forest, in which many species of bird may be seen, to the unwooded top of Cragan Liath Mor from where you may obtain good views in all directions. Loch Tummel lies to the

Loch Tummel.

south-east, Loch Rannoch to the south-west, and the 3,520-feet peak of Schiehallion rises beyond them.

The first one and a quarter miles of the walk westward rises some 350 feet or so towards Torr Dubh. The track then makes a sharp left-hand bend to continue east across the slopes of the hills for another one and a quarter miles, crossing three streams. It then climbs gently to the summit. The total length of the walk up to the top is just over three miles, and the path rises just over 700 feet in all.

16.   THE LOCH CON MURDER
Loch Errochty

Loch Errochty, which lies remote and solitary among heather-covered hills between Loch Rannoch and Glen Garry, is today a larger sheet of water than it was in the time of the legend we are about to recount. A great hydroelectric dam has been built across Errochty Water, which flows out of the loch and down Glen Errochty to join the River Garry. Behind the dam, the valley of the river has filled to increase the size of the loch.

The dam across Errochty Water.

North of Loch Errochty lies little Loch Con, bleak and lonely among the heather and scrub. The Allt Con, which once flowed south from Loch Con to join Errochty Water, now flows into Loch Errochty. It was in Loch Con that the murderous climax to our legend took place.

Dhonnoch Reamhar, 'Stout Duncan', was a kinsman of the McDonalds of Glengarry who had come into possession of lands in Argyle and Ross as a result of his marriage to a daughter of the Lord of the Isles.

Having gained possession of the lands Duncan, who by all accounts was a wild character, proceeded to ignore his wife's existence. He was often away on raids against other clans and when he was not plundering them he enjoyed his ill-gotten gains in the company of other women.

It is said that once in his younger days, when pursued by some angry victims, he came to a steep cliff at the edge of Errochty Water and seeing there was no escape, gambled his life on being able to leap across the gap to the other bank. He succeeded and the place where he made his prodigious leap is still known as Dhonnoch Reamhar's Leap. You can visit the place by following the valley from the River Errochty.

Though Duncan ignored his wife, she, being a daughter of a proud clan, did not accept such treatment easily and showed her resentment in every way possible, to such an extent that it was a subject of gossip far and wide.

This was a source of constant irritation to Duncan. He could not forget the fact that he owed much of his land to his wife and that if her father felt it necessary to interfere in their altercations on her behalf it would have a disadvantageous result for him. Duncan eventually decided that the only way to prevent this happening was to get rid of his wife permanently.

He thought about various ways of achieving this end, but none of them satisfied him. Those which involved the collaboration of servants to do the deed were too likely to be discovered owing to the inability of servants to keep

113

secrets, and any in which only he himself was involved presented the problem of how to deal with the body once he had murdered his wife.

Duncan spent days wandering over the countryside turning the matter over in his mind and his lengthy presence at their home lulled his wife into the belief that Duncan had begun to change his ways. When, therefore, her husband suggested one day that they take a walk up the valley to Loch Con, a lonely and isolated loch in which there stood a small island with a cave among its rocks, the poor lady agreed with alacrity.

To reach the loch Duncan and his wife walked up Errochty Water and then turned up a small steep-sided valley that led to the loch. When they had reached it, Duncan suggested that they should visit the island and, boarding a boat that he previously left among some rocks, he rowed his wife across to the island. He then told her about the secret cave that he had discovered and wondered if it was one of the abodes of the Little People that the country folk believed in.

While his wife was peering into the darkness of the cave Duncan came up behind her and struck her a blow across the back of the head which rendered her instantly unconscious. Duncan rapidly bundled her into the cave and began to throw rocks against the entrance. He was a powerful man and he had no fears at all that his wife would be able to pull the stones away. Having completed his grim task, Duncan rowed himself back to the shore and returned to his castle.

Duncan himself never returned to the spot. In a few years the blocked cave was completely overgrown with weeds and brambles and no one would have guessed that under the greenery there lay the body of the daughter of the Lord of the Isles and the wife of Duncan Dhonnoch Reamhar. Over the years, however, stories have been told by visitors to the area of ghostly sightings and the wailing and sighing of a woman's voice. Surely they can only be of the long-dead lady who was entombed by her husband more than two hundred years ago.

THE WALK:	MAP SQUARE:
FROM TRINAFOUR TO LOCH CON AND BACK.	Ordnance Survey Sheet 42/728646 A relatively easy 7-mile walk to the scene of the crime.

Trinafour, start of the walk here, is a small village at the head of Glen Errochty, lying on the B847, mid-way between Calvine off the A9 and Drumglas near Kinloch Rannoch.

Trinafour is suggested as the start of the walk rather than the gate to the private road which leads directly to Loch Con, because the latter lies on a hairpin bend leaving no room for convenient parking.

This walk is remarkable more for its splendid solitude than for any particular grandeur of scenery or interesting sights. You will not be able to retrace Duncan's last walk with his wife, as he probably followed the natural route up Errochty Water and the Allt Con, part of which the dam has now drowned.

Beginning at Trinafour, then, you follow the minor road marked 'Dalnacardoch' out of the village. This narrow, winding and steep road goes up Errochty Water for about a quarter of a mile before climbing uphill away from the river then making a sharp left-hand turning near a copse of trees towards Errochty Dam. About half a mile from Trinafour, you will pass a private road to the dam. Another half mile will bring you to another gate marked 'private' at a point where the road makes a sharp hairpin bend uphill. The track on the other side of this gate is your way to Loch Con.

Ahead of you, a line of electricity pylons march across the heather-covered land. To the left of the picture stands the impressive shape of Errochty Dam, and stretching away in all directions are heather and grass-covered slopes whose only inhabitants seem to be sheep cropping the scrub.

The walk from the gate to Loch Con is about two and three-quarter miles. In front of you for much of it you will have the 1,840 feet peak of Sron Chon which sits between Loch Con and the larger Loch Errochty to the south. Further south, beyond Loch Errochty, the much higher Beinn a' Chullaich (2,896 feet) dominates the skyline. The track is relatively easy, following a steady rise until it reaches the loch which sits in a depression in the hills.

17. THE GHOST OF KILLIECRANKIE
The Pass of Killiecrankie, Perthshire

The Pass of Killiecrankie is a beautiful wooded place, with a deep ravine through which the River Garry pours in a torrent as it heads for the Falls of Tummel and Loch Faskally. Above the Pass lies Blair Castle at Blair Atholl (open daily from May to mid-October) and below, three miles to the south, is Pitlochry. Pleasantly sited on the north bank of Tummel the town is well known for its annual drama festival and also for the unusual fish pass at the southern end of Loch Faskally, which enables visitors to see the salmon as they head up river for the spawning season.

All this area is famous for its scenery, and even without its historical interest the Pass of Killiecrankie would rank high among the attractions of this part of the Grampians region.

In July of 1689 the Pass was the scene of a battle between the forces of William III of Orange, and the Scots who supported the deposed Stuarts under Graham Claverhouse, Viscount Dundee, whose popularity had earned him the nickname of Bonnie Dundee. The war between the English forces and the Jacobite Scots, mostly Highlanders, who remained loyal to the Stuart king had reached a critical point, with General Mackay, who commanded the government troops, attempting to pin down and destroy the Scots and Bonnie Dundee. To do this, Mackay decided he must take Blair Castle, a chief stronghold of the Earls and Dukes of Athol, from which General Montrose had set out in his daring campaign against Argyle in an earlier period of the struggle.

Hearing of Mackay's intentions, Dundee marched his men quickly to the head of the Killiecrankie Pass through which Mackay's troops would have to go. On the eve of the battle, he pitched his tents in the hills above the valley and surveyed the scene.

Overhead, the sky glittered with stars and below the earth was dark and silent, except for the occasional murmur of his soldiers talking to each other as they prepared themselves for the next day's affray. At the end of the valley Dundee could just make out the dark masses of trees at the beginnings of the pass. He was well placed, he thought, to take Mackay's troops by surprise as soon as they appeared at the point where the pass opened out into the valley. Having satisfied himself that he had taken every possibility into account, Dundee went to his tent and settled himself down to sleep.

In the middle of the night he woke with a start. A figure stood at the end of his bed and Dundee thought at first that it was one of his own soldiers. The apparition was a tall man in Highland dress. His face was pale and there was a gash across his forehead from which blood flowed and congealed over the eye and cheekbone. As Dundee was about to question the figure, he found himself suddenly looking into empty darkness. No one was there. He called out then to his guard, asking him if he had seen anyone enter, but the guard had seen nothing. Thinking that he must have been dreaming Dundee lay down once more to sleep.

The second time he awoke and saw the apparition Dundee knew this was no real person, but must be some figment of his imagination. Being a practical man, he closed his mind to any superstitious fears and dismissed the incident from his thoughts as soon as the vision faded. The third time the ghost appeared, Dundee knew that he had to accept that this was a supernatural visitor and ordered him to make his purpose clear. The ghost's eyes seemed to be trying to communicate a message but nothing was said; then he raised an arm and pointed in the direction of the next day's field of battle.

Dundee felt a sudden alarm and when the ghost had gone the word 'Tomorrow' repeated itself over and over in his mind.

Before noon the following day, Mackay's men began to appear at the entrance to the pass but Dundee withheld the order to attack. His men looked at him anxiously, eager to begin the battle. A few desultory shots picked out one or two of the enemy who hid among the rocks in the pass and returned the fire. Dundee ignored his officers' demands for permission to attack, appearing preoccupied throughout the day. Finally, as the pass began to darken in the evening light, he ordered a charge.

The Highlanders poured down the hill, their pent-up impatience bursting out with a ferocity that confused and frightened Mackay's troops, who turned and tried to find shelter in the pass once more. In the excitement of the battle, Dundee forgot his visitor of the previous night. He swept down with his troops on to the enemy, urging his men on to make a quick end to the battle. Success, he knew, was in his grasp – but as the conviction formed in his mind, he felt a blow in his side and fell headlong on the grass. A shot from a retreating English soldier had fatally wounded him and in a few moments he was dead.

Dundee's death did more than fulfil the prediction of his ghostly visitor, for it put an end, for a while at any rate, to any hopes that James II or his son, the so-called Old Pretender, would occupy again the thrones of Scotland and England. Without a leader like Dundee, there was no one to rally the loyal Highlanders, until the young Prince Charles Edward Stuart made a final and tragic attempt to claim the throne on his father's behalf in 1745.

THE WALK:
FROM THE VISITOR
CENTRE AT KILLIE-
CRANKIE ALONG THE
RIVER GARRY TO THE
RIVER TUMMEL AND
BACK.

MAP SQUARE:
Ordnance Survey Sheet
43/917627
A good walk, of about 4¼
miles in all, with several
points of interest on the
way.

*The Pass of Killiecrankie lies on the A9 from Stirling to
John O'Groat's, a fine, wide road, with numerous dual-
carriageway sections. The nearest town, Pitlochry, has many
good shops and hotels, and at Killiecrankie itself there is a
hotel. The National Trust for Scotland maintains a fine
Visitor Centre, attractively situated at the top of the pass,
where there is a parking area, a good book shop, and displays
about the pass and its history.*

*The walk starts from the Visitor Centre. Following the path
behind the building, you walk down the steep ravine to the*

The Pass of Killiecrankie.

River Garry, where the path leads down to the narrowest part of the ravine. At the bottom are the great water-splashed rocks known as the Soldier's Leap, after the exploit of one of the fleeing English soldiers who, finding himself closely pursued, leapt eighteen feet across the torrent of the River Garry rather then be captured by the Scots.

The path now descends to river level under the railway viaduct and continues along the wooded banks of the river to a wooden footbridge, less than three-quarters of a mile from the start, which takes you into the Tummel woods. You are now on the west bank of the river and your path will soon be joined by the path that descends from the new bridge which takes the Loch Rannoch road off the A9.

The path now goes on for another three-quarters of a mile to the confluence of the River Garry and the River Tummel. There is a waterfall here and a pass allowing the salmon to swim upstream to spawn. The scenery is delightful at this point, with wooded hills and towering peaks converging on the meeting of the rivers.

You can go a little further up the Tummel valley and then return along the upper path to the Garry River valley and the Pass of Killiecrankie, the whole walk being about four and a quarter miles.

18. THE MONSTER OF THE DEE
Braemar

Braemar is situated in the upper course of the Dee 1,100 feet above sea level. The village is surrounded by wooded hills that shelter it from the winds, especially in winter when snow blankets the surrounding hills. It is a popular resort and the setting for the well-known Braemar Gathering, or Highland Games, held every autumn.

The River Dee, into which flows Clunie Water at Braemar, is a fine fishing river and provides a lovely setting for such famous buildings as Balmoral Castle and Braemar Castle. Several islands dot the waters of the Dee, on one of which, legend has it, Malcolm III (Canmore) kept a monster. Historically it is probable that Malcolm Canmore occupied Kindrochit Castle which once stood near Clunie Bridge in Braemar. As for the monster . . .

This creature apparently had a voracious appetite and Malcolm Canmore was hard put to find the money with which to buy its food. Though almost eaten out of house and home by the beast, Malcolm Canmore would not get rid of it, for the King was irrationally fond of his strange pet. He cast around for a means of raising the money required for the animal's upkeep and, like most people in positions of authority, he came to the conclusion that the only way to do this was to impose a tax on the local peasants.

Most of the peasants grumbled but paid up, except for an old lady called MacLeod who felt that the tax being levied on her in order to keep the creature fed could quite properly be described as monstrous. She therefore refused to pay it. This annoyed Malcolm Canmore, who

122

determined to get his money and teach the old girl a lesson at the same time. He ordered all the woman's worldly goods to be seized. As it happened, the MacLeod woman's worldly goods consisted of one cow, without which she would have had no source of income at all.

Extremely upset by Canmore's hard-heartedness, the MacLeod lady sent a message to her son telling him of her predicament. Young MacLeod immediately came to his mother's rescue. Reasoning that if there were no monster there would be no need to raise a tax to feed it, he shot it with his bow and arrow.

As soon as he heard of the fate of his pet, the distressed and angry Malcolm Canmore ordered the young MacLeod to be seized and brought to him. His intention was to have the young man sentenced to death immediately and he was in the middle of pronouncing the sentence when young MacLeod's wife and son appeared, interrupting the court's proceedings to beg for Malcolm Canmore's mercy.

The King had no intention of showing any compassion to the man who had killed his favourite monster, but his eye was caught by a large wheat bannock that MacLeod's son was stuffing into his mouth, and the thought came to him then that death might be too easy a punishment for MacLeod; perhaps he would suffer more if he were to see his son and heir in mortal danger, especially if the responsibility for the son's fate rested with the father.

Malcolm Canmore therefore changed the sentence to one of death, or to freedom – if MacLeod could shoot a bannock off his son's head at fifty paces. Curiously enough this feet was performed later in Switzerland by a certain William Tell, though with an apple instead of a bannock. MacLeod did not know that he was creating a precedent but as he was the best bowman on the Dee and, encouraged by his wife and son, he decided to have a try to win his life and freedom.

The young boy was placed at a distance of fifty paces and a bannock balanced on his head. Calmly, he stood waiting his father's shot. As MacLeod raised the bow and squinted along the arrow – the bannock seemed very small. He took a deep breath, prayed hard and let the arrow fly. All the spectators held their breath and then expelled it in a cry of delight as the arrow split the bannock in two and then continued on its course, finally coming to rest in a tree.

MacLeod ran to his son and, gathering him up, left the glen with his wife – a free man.

THE WALKS:

1. FROM INVERCAULD HOUSE, EAST OF BRAEMAR TO THE LINN OF QUOICH.

2. FROM VICTORIA BRIDGE, ON THE LINN OF DEE ROAD, TO THE LINN OF QUOICH.

MAP SQUARE:

1. Ordnance Survey Sheet 43/174924

2. Ordnance Survey Sheet 43/102896

Two walks, a longish one of about 7 miles and a shorter one of about 4 miles, both to the Linn of Quoich, to introduce you to the beauties of Royal Deeside.

Braemar lies on the A93 from Perth to Aberdeen, which runs along Glen Clunie. There is no railway to Braemar, but a bus service operates from Perth.

Royal Deeside became a popular summer resort when Queen Victoria and Prince Albert made their summer home at Balmoral, and continues in popularity with visitors today. The Royal Family still enjoy their summer holidays at Balmoral Castle, the grounds of which are open to the public daily during May, June and July, except when members of the

Royal Family are in residence.

On the outskirts of Braemar is Braemar Castle, built by the Earl of Mar early in the seventeenth century. This turreted tower castle has been in the possession of the Farquharsons of Invercauld since 1731. It can be visited daily from May to October.

The valleys and wooded hillsides around Braemar provide numerous pleasant walks, though care must be taken in the stalking season, when private estates may not want walkers on their land. A particularly popular destination for local walks is the Linn of Quoich, where Quoich Water flows into the River Dee.

Our FIRST SUGGESTED WALK to the Linn of Quoich starts from another historic home in the area, Invercauld House which lies to the east of Braemar on the north bank of the River Dee. Invercauld House dates back to the fifteenth

Braemar.

century, and it was from here that the Earl of Mar called out the clans in support of the Old Pretender in 1715.

To reach the house, leave Braemar on the A93 in the direction of Balmoral, and cross the Dee at Invercauld Bridge. You can leave your car here or drive east to Invercauld House (which is not open to the public) and start your walk from this point.

After about a quarter of a mile, the road crosses the Alltdourie and here you should branch off the road (which goes to the houses and other buildings at Alltdourie) and take the track which runs along the low-lying ground between the woodland here and the Dee. After approximately three-quarters of a mile, you will pass the cottage at Ballnagower on your right, with Braemar Castle standing proudly on the opposite side of the river to your left.

Another two and a half miles of pleasant walking, with splendid views of hill and woodland all round, and Braemar village nestling on the opposite bank of the Dee, brings you to Allanaquoich and the Linn of Quoich. 'Quoich' means 'cup' in Gaelic, and refers to the large potholes the falling water has gouged out of the rocks.

For the SECOND SUGGESTED (SHORTER) WALK, drive westward out of Braemar on the Linn of Dee road, and cross to the north side of the river at Victoria Bridge, just four miles from Braemar. Leaving the car here, you can walk to the Linn of Quoich – about two miles on.

19. THE WITCH OF MAR
Abergeldie Castle near Braemar

Abergeldie Castle, near Braemar, is a delightfully domestic-looking building today. An apricot-pink colour, and with an informal garden surrounding it, this typically Scottish tower house would hardly warrant the grand title 'castle' but for the fact that it was once lived in by Edward VII and Queen Alexandra when they were Prince and Princess of Wales. It is still leased today by the Queen from its owners, the Gordons of Huntly, who were also at one time the owners of the Balmoral Estate, which Prince Albert bought in 1852.

Abergeldie Castle, which is private and not open to the public, lies on the south bank of the Dee, two miles east of Balmoral Castle. It dates from the mid-sixteenth century, though there are nineteenth-century additions. It is from the earlier period of the castle's history that our legend dates.

It was a time when witches might still be found living in most villages, ready to cast spells involving eye of toad and tongue of newt and other nasty ingredients. One such witch lived near Abergeldie Castle. She was so old that no one knew her age or could recall a time when she had not been living alone and solitary in her tumble-down cottage in the forest near the castle. She was clearly eccentric in her ways, and had long been known as 'the witch of Mar'. Her sole companion was a large ginger cat whose bright yellow eyes frightened the local children almost as much as did the old woman herself.

Not that the children had much to do with her; they had learned from the other villagers to keep away from her. So the old woman lived very much alone, talking to few beyond her cat and, no doubt, 'familiars' and creatures who move by night whom witches were known to prefer to ordinary folk. The villagers were sure that every time a cow died, a hen stopped laying, the milk turned sour or some natural disaster struck the village, it meant that the old woman had been practising her evil spells again.

One day, as the old woman bent over the great cooking pot, or cauldron, which always hung steaming over the fire, she heard footsteps behind her, and turned round just as a figure stepped over her threshold. Its outline darkened the doorway so that the old figure had to peer to see who her unexpected — and unwelcome — visitor might be.

As the figure stepped nearer the firelight, the old witch recognized the wife of the Laird of Abergeldie. 'This is a strange place for the lady of Abergeldie to come to,' cried the Witch of Mar. 'What do you want with me?'

The lady of Abergeldie seemed tense and distracted. She clasped and unclasped her fingers round the leather purse she carried, then she said in a rush, 'My husband is unfaithful to me, I know he is. I believe he wants to turn me off and wed another. I want you to look into the future. If there is a woman coming to supplant me, I must know of it.'

She tipped gold coins from her purse and held them out to the Witch of Mar.

'Your lord has been away from Abergeldie Castle for many months, lady,' said the old woman, who missed nothing of what was going on among the local people. 'How do you know he is unfaithful to you?'

'He has been in France too long,' the jealous and angry lady of Abergeldie replied. 'I know he has found someone else at the French court! I know it! Tell me!'

The old woman looked at the lady, then at the gold she was offering, and, turning to her fire, added more fuel to it.

Soon the cauldron hanging above it was steaming hot, and the witch of Mar began throwing in strange ingredients: the leg of a dead cat, crackling dried plants, dried toad powder, pieces of tree bark and other weird things.

The two women sat mesmerized staring into the cauldron, the old crone muttering strange words over and over again, until the steam rising from the cauldron began to change colour and assume odd shapes. Then, as the lady Abergeldie gazed fearfully at it, the steam turned vivid scarlet and assumed the form of two people. One was a woman, young, shapely and comely; the other was a man. They stood side by side on the deck of a ship.

The lady of Abergeldie jumped to her feet, her eyes blazing with jealous fury. 'I knew it! Oh, that you could raise a storm to wreck that ship and drown so faithless a husband!' she cried. 'There will be more gold for you if you can cast such a spell.'

The witch of Mar demurred at first, then agreed to come to Abergeldie Castle and cast a spell which would rid the lady of Abergeldie of her husband. Pausing only to hide away the gold the lady had given her, the witch followed her back to Abergeldie. The two women climbed to a lonely room at the top of the highest tower in the castle and there the witch of Mar began weaving a new spell.

First, she laid a basin of water on the table in front of her, then she floated a shallow dish in the centre of the water. Finally, she ordered the lady of Abergeldie to sit down and watch the basin, never taking her eyes off it, while she herself found a dark corner in the deepest vault of the castle, and drew herself into it. There she crouched, keening and moaning to herself, on and on in an endless chant that utterly terrified the castle servants who heard it.

Meanwhile, alone at the top of the tower, the lady of Abergeldie watched the basin. The water in it began to quiver slightly, then to move more and more violently until it was slopping over the sides, splashing the table and causing the dish floating in the centre to tip crazily from side to side. Finally, one last violent heave of the water tipped the dish over completely, and it sank like a stone to the bottom of the basin. The water became still again.

The terrible significance of what she had seen jerked the lady of Abergeldie to her feet – and to her senses. She ran down the tower steps, to be brought up short in the castle courtyard by the old woman.

'It is done, lady. Your husband will never come back to Abergeldie.' The old woman turned and walked out of the castle.

The lady of Abergeldie was horrified at what she had done. Her jealous rage completely gone, she spent many hours on her knees over the next few days praying for the safe return of her husband.

Then came the news she had dreaded: the Laird of Abergeldie, returning to Scotland from France, had drowned when his ship had foundered with all hands.

The lady of Abergeldie sent men to kill the witch of Mar, but they found no one in her home, only a great ginger cat and a sleek black one which ran into the forest as the men approached with lighted torches to destroy the cottage and all its contents.

As the men watched the flames engulf the cottage, they saw the black cat leap from a branch, heard it laugh a wailing, cackling laugh in the voice of the witch of Mar, then saw it disappear into the forest, never to be seen again.

THE WALK:
FROM BALMORAL
CASTLE TO ABERGELDIE
CASTLE.

MAP SQUARE:
Ordnance Survey Sheet
44/264950
A short and easy walk
– 4 miles for the round walk –
along a pretty country road.

Abergeldie Castle.

*Abergeldie Castle lies on the B927 which is a turning marked
'South Deeside' off the Braemar–Ballater section of the A93
at Balmoral Castle.*

*You can leave your car in the car park by the A93, then
walk across the bridge over the Dee. The main gate to
Balmoral Castle grounds is on your right, and the B976 turns
left.*

*Balmoral Castle grounds are open to the public in May,
June and July, daily except Sundays, unless members of the
Royal Family are in residence, so you may want to visit them
before walking on to Abergeldie.*

*The two-mile walk to Abergeldie along the B976 is easy and
pleasant. To your left, the broad River Dee flows in its shallow
stony bed, and you will have frequent glimpses of it through
the trees and bushes which edge its banks. On your right, for
much of your walk, you will be able to see into the grounds of
Balmoral Castle.*

*Abergeldie is not on the grand scale like Balmoral or
Braemar Castle. You will find an attractive little tower
castle, topped with a cupola and a gold weather vane.*

20. THE BURIAL AT CARRBRIDGE
Carrbridge

After passing Aviemore, the A9 climbs over hills to the valley of the River Dulnain. Hills dotted with patches of trees and heather and a patchwork of fields stretch away in every direction from the village that lies across the river. In winter Carrbridge is a skiing centre giving access to the Cairngorms and in summer visitors come for the golf or walks in the hills. The Landmark Visitor Centre has a nature trail and an audio-visual theatre which presents a programme of two thousand years of Scottish history.

Today the road traffic crosses the River Dulnain by a modern bridge. Next to it upstream stands a ruined arch, the remains of the old bridge built by the Earl of Seafield in 1717 in order, it is said, to give access to the cemetery when the river was in flood. Previously, there had been only a ford across the river.

The story of how the bridge came to be built seems to bear out the reason given for its construction.

There once lived in Carrbridge an old lady who, as she grew even older, began to fret about her last resting place. In particular, she was concerned that her funeral procession might not be able to ford the boulder-strewn River Dunain if it happened to be in spate at the time of her death.

Day after day, she confessed her anxiety to her friends and neighbours, until they were all tired of hearing about it, especially as she did not appear in imminent danger of death. Eventually, to stop her insistent demands that whatever the state of the river she would be buried at the cemetery and nowhere else, her neighbours agreed amongst themselves to tell a white lie and promise that somehow or other they would get her coffin across the river.

'Mind,' the old lady said, 'a promise is a promise and you must take my coffin down to the river, whatever its state.'

Well, the old lady died soon after having extracted this promise from her neighbours, but when the time came for transporting her coffin to the cemetery there seemed little chance of its being kept, for the river was in flood.

Some of the mourners who had volunteered to carry the coffin voiced the opinion that they might as well forget any attempt to get the coffin across the river because it was running too fast and deep; others felt guilty at breaking their word. They agreed that it was impossible to cross the river at that time, but they felt that if they carried the coffin down to the water's edge they would at least have shown that they had tried.

After a short discussion, the other mourners fell in with this suggestion. Picking up the coffin, which was quite light, for the old lady had been rather frail, they walked slowly down to the river with the rest of the villagers following behind.

At the river's edge they looked across towards the cemetery and knew that there was no hope of crossing over to it for several days. They were just about to turn back to the village when to their astonishment they saw the swollen torrent of the river begin to recede on each side of the ford, leaving a clear way across which they could walk.

At first, no one moved, but as the water level fell lower and lower the leader of the men carrying the coffin called out to the others to make a dash for it while they could. When they were about halfway across the mourners noticed that in the walls of water to each side of them were scores of salmon that, finding their progress up river interrupted, were jumping into the dry lane and thrashing about in their efforts to return to their more usual element.

Seeing this unexpected windfall of fish, the mourners flung themselves on to their knees, attempting to catch the slippery creatures. Soon, they were joined in the hunt by the men carrying the coffin, who did not see why they should not take advantage of this unexpected opportunity to take home a nice fresh salmon for tea.

No sooner had the men laid the coffin down than the waters closed with a terrible crash, sending the mourners tumbling over and over among the rocks and drowning not a few of them. The rest scrambled ashore and lay gasping for breath on the river bank stunned by these unexpected events.

Chastened by their experience, the villagers swore that they would build a bridge across to the cemetery so the dead might be buried in dignity whatever the river was like, and that is the bridge whose remains you may see at Carrbridge today.

And as for the old lady? Possibly embarrassed, the tellers of the story give no details. One hopes her coffin was eventually laid to rest in the cemetery.

THE WALK:	MAP SQUARE:
FROM THE OLD BRIDGE AT CARRBRIDGE TO SLUGGAN BRIDGE, AND BACK.	Ordnance Survey Sheet 36/907229 An interesting walk of about 4 miles through an open valley and farming country.

Carrbridge lies just off the A9 between Aviemore and Inverness; the River Dulnain, on which stand both the eighteenth-century bridges which feature in the walk here, flows through the centre of the village.

The walk starts on the south bank of the river, and takes

The Bridge at Carrbridge.

you along the minor road signposted 'Dalnahaitnach'. You will see first the high arch of the ruined bridge, in a picturesque setting over the boulder-strewn river bed where the water tumbles and gurgles. Trees line the banks of the river, and small cottages nestle above. A hundred yards or so past the bridge, the Carrbridge cemetery and war memorial are in a grove of conifers on the left of the road.

From here, the walk takes you under the railway line and the A9, past guest houses, a timber mill and an eyesore of a car dump, and out into the countryside where the land is at first prettily wooded and then becomes more open and heather covered.

Just about two miles from the start of the walk, you will come to two gates, one on each side of the road, and each marked 'private'. The walk takes you through the right-hand gate – it is all right to walk up this grassy track but not, of course, to take a car up it – to the Old Sluggan Bridge over the River Dulnain just under half a mile further on.

The bridge stands on a bend in the river in a copse of trees. There are a few houses nearby. The bridge was built early in the eighteenth century to carry one of General Wade's military roads, which linked Inverness garrison with Ruthven Barracks near Kingussie, over the Dulnain.

You can walk back to Carrbridge by the same road you came out of the village on, which, because it is quite high up, gives you good views of Carrbridge and the surrounding hills as you approach it.

Alternatively, you can cross Sluggan Bridge and turn right on to a path over the fields back to Carrbridge. After about one and a quarter miles, this path becomes a narrow road passing under the A9 and the railway, bringing you back into the village to the north of the river.

21. THE BATTLE OF CULLODEN
Culloden Moor

The quiet and rather bleak fields of Culloden Moor, five miles east of Inverness, make up probably the most evocative place in all Scotland. Here, in just forty minutes of desperate fighting on 16 April 1746, the most romantic and ill-fated venture ever undertaken on behalf of the deposed Stuart rulers of Scotland, came to a tragic end.

Culloden was the last battle to be fought on British soil and the Moor itself became the graveyard for some 1,200 gallant Highlanders and just 76 of George II's troops.

Today, the Moor is, not surprisingly, a major tourist attraction, and the National Trust for Scotland has its usual excellent Visitor Centre to provide all the information you may require, at the same time using various kinds of display to re-create the events of a venture which, while its historical facts are well enough known, has provided the stuff for many a legend.

Prince Charles Edward Stuart had landed in Scotland eight months before, to raise the Highlanders on behalf of his father, the Old Pretender (James VIII). His venture was rash, ill-timed and ill-prepared. The backing he had hoped for from the French had failed to materialize; money, men and arms were all desperately insufficient for his purpose. The wonder is that he achieved so much.

Prince Charles raised his father's standard at Glenfinnan on 19 August 1745 and enough Highlanders rallied to his cause to take him in some triumph to Edinburgh and armed success at Prestonpans. In November, he headed south over the Border, and had reached Derby by the beginning of December. In London, George II was considering calling up the royal yacht so that he could flee to Hanover, but very few English had rallied to the cause of the Stuarts, and on 4 December Prince Charles ordered his forces to retreat to Scotland.

Bonnie Prince Charlie was not yet defeated. He had his first encounter with the Duke of Cumberland, George II's twenty-four-year-old son and commander of the King's troops, at Clifton Moor near Penrith and at least checked the Duke's advance. He entered Glasgow on 26 December, forcing from the reluctant town a Christmas gift of £10,000, and won another battle at Falkirk on 17 January. His army failed to take Stirling Castle, however, and dispirited, it retreated to Inverness where it arrived on 18 February. Here, the Prince's army, or what was left of it, awaited the advance of the Duke of Cumberland.

There was no money to pay the Highlanders, and food was desperately short; as the weeks passed the Prince's army began to melt away, so that by mid-April he had only 5,000 ill-equipped men to confront Cumberland's 9,000, who were backed up by artillery and cavalry.

Cumberland set up camp at Nairn and was in fine enough fettle to spend the day before the battle celebrating his birthday with his troops. The Highlanders, on the other hand, spent it on a mistaken march to try for a night attack against Cumberland's army, ten miles away at Nairn. The distance was too great, and at dawn on 16 April they had to turn back towards Culloden Moor.

Consequently, it was a tired, hungry and dispirited little army who drew themselves up to face Cumberland later in the day. It was not even complete, for some of them were away foraging for food, and the Prince, desperate for money, had sent another 1,500 north to try to recover the gold and supplies lost from the Jacobite ship *Hasard* aground in the Kyle of Tongue.

The two armies were drawn up 400 or 500 yards apart,

Cumberland's troops in three lines. At one in the afternoon, he opened up with an artillery barrage then the Highlanders fearlessly charged the troops before them. They succeeded in breaking the first line before being utterly overwhelmed. Forty minutes after it had begun, the battle was over. Twelve hundred Highlanders were either dead or wounded, the latter soon to be butchered on the field or in the surrounding woods, Cumberland having ordered that the wounded were not to be spared. Of Cumberland's own forces, only 76 were killed on the field, and another 230 or so were wounded.

After the battle, Prince Charles Edward Stuart spent five months as a fugitive in the Highlands and Islands of Scotland. There was a price of £30,000 on his head – an enormous sum in those days – but no one betrayed him. In September, he finally boarded a French ship at a spot not far from where he had landed the year before, and was taken back to France. His Rising was over.

The Duke of Cumberland's repression had only begun. The policy of root-and-branch vengeance he followed in the Highlands, marked as it was by plunder, murder and a terrible inhumanity, is remembered to this day. Not for nothing was he nicknamed 'Butcher'. The English down south might sing 'Hail the Conquering Hero Comes', composed for the occasion by Handel, and name a flower Sweet William in his honour; to the Scots, his memorial is a weed called Sticking Billy.

THE WALKS:

1. THE CULLODEN MOOR
   BATTLEFIELD WALK.

MAP SQUARE:
Ordnance Survey Sheets:
1. 27/745450

2. THE CULLODEN
   FOREST TRAIL.

2. 27/714458
The first walk here is an easy,
one-mile walk round the
main points of interest on the
battlefield; the second is
also not difficult, and follows
a 2 mile-long prepared
forest path.

*Culloden Moor lies along the B9006 between Inverness and
Nairn, off the A96(T), a main trunk road, from which
Culloden may also be reached via several roads turning off
south of Inverness.*

*Our FIRST SUGGESTED WALK at Culloden is the
Battlefield Trail which has been laid out on the site. The Trail
actually starts about half a mile to the west of the Visitor*

The Cumberland Stone, Culloden Moor.

Centre, but we suggest you go to the Centre first. There is a car park here, and in the shop you will find booklets and maps of the battle.

The Battlefield Trail circles the area of the main battle and takes you over the front lines of both forces. You will be following stone walls which were not on the Moor in 1746. Old Leanach Cottage, on the other hand, which is now a NTS information centre and museum, did exist in 1746; the battle actually raged around it. From the cottage a path crosses the Field of the English where Cumberland's dead were buried.

The Trail will also take you past the tall Cairn on the north side of the B9006, erected in 1881 to commemorate the fallen. Near it, on both sides of the road, are stones marking the graves of the Highlanders, buried according to their clans.

To the east, beyond the Visitor Centre, is the Cumberland Stone, a large boulder on which the Duke of Cumberland is supposed to have stood to watch the course of the battle. Three hundred yards to the north is the Well of the Dead, at which wounded Highlanders were killed while trying to drink the water.

Our SECOND SUGGESTED WALK in the area of Culloden is the lovely Forest Trail which has been laid out two miles north of the battlefield. You reach it via the A96(T) from Inverness, taking a right turn off the road towards Smithton just two miles out of Inverness. The Trail begins at the T-junction you come to in another three-quarters of a mile.

This is a two-mile walk, carefully posted to show the forest together with the different species of tree as well as the plants and animals which live in it.

There is a car park, and a map board.

22. THE GHOST OF RAIT CASTLE
Nairn

Nairn is an attractive town at the mouth of the River Nairn, where it flows into the Moray Firth. It is surrounded by low wooded hills and farmland among which are a number of sites of historical importance; south-west of the town is Balblair, where the Duke of Cumberland camped before Culloden; to the east is Hardmuir, the blasted heath where Macbeth met the three witches. Macbeth's castle, Cawdor, is only five miles to the south on the A9090.

In the hills south of Nairn lie the ruins of Rait Castle, a fourteenth-century building with a macabre history and a ghost that is supposed to haunt it to this day, a sad relic of an appalling day in 1414 when the Comyn (Cummings) owners of Rait Castle were massacred by the Mackintoshes.

The master of Rait Castle at that time, chief of the Cummings, was a dour and severe man who would never let his daughter out of his sight. Since he had to make business journeys away from the castle every now and again, it was impossible for him to keep her permanently under surveillance and as she grew up she began to meet some of the young men who lived in the neighbourhood. One of them happened to be from the Mackintosh clan, her father's enemies.

The chief of the Cummings had long harboured a grievance against the Mackintoshes, a grievance which he soon discovered was shared by other members of his clan. It did not take long for the chief and his clansmen to move on from this discovery to plotting how they might destroy the Mackintosh clan. As in so many Highland conflicts, this one was to be resolved by violence, with the Mackintoshes being taken by surprise. To this end the Chief of the Cummings pretended to be friendly to his enemies and even invited them to meet him at an inn on neutral ground: there would be eating and drinking with past differences drowned in a friendly toast.

On the evening of the planned massacre, everything went well and to an outsider it might have looked as if the long rivalry between the Cummings and the Mackintoshes was over. The Cummings were biding their time. As the appointed hour approached, every Cummings man carried on drinking and chatting with nervous anticipation. In that last hour before the signal was to be given the minutes dragged interminably by. As the candles on the table guttered on their spires of melted wax, the Cummings prepared . . . then, so suddenly that they were taken completely by surprise, they found themselves at the mercy of the daggers that the Mackintoshes had suddenly pulled out from their hiding places among their clothes.

In wild disbelief, those who could do so dived for the doors and windows, bleeding from the wounds that their foes had given them at the first onslaught. Those Cummings who were trapped in the room were mercilessly slaughtered by their intended victims.

One of those who managed to escape was the Cummings Chief, swearing to find and punish the man who had betrayed him. However, his efforts to discover his betrayer led him to a conclusion that filled him with horror. According to local gossip his daughter had been seen talking with increasing frequency to a Mackintosh lad. The day before the ill-fated meeting in the inn the youth had been seen riding away from Rait Castle.

The Cummings Chief had sworn to punish the betrayer and he now carried out his oath. He found his daughter at the top of the castle's round tower where she was spinning.

Shouting that he knew about her treachery and how she had betrayed the Cummings plan in order to save her lover's life, he pinned her to the ground and severed both her hands.

As she staggered down the tower's steps after this bloody and terrible deed, the Chief of the Cummings heard a piercing cry and then silence. His daughter, unable to stand the physical pain and mental anguish caused by her father's attack on her, had jumped out of the window and killed herself.

Her ghost haunts the castle still, but whether in expiation of the betrayal of her father's clan or in mute protest at her innocence, nobody knows.

Ruins of Rait Castle near Nairn.

THE WALK:
FROM THE B9109 TO
RAIT CASTLE.

MAP SQUARE:
Ordnance Survey Sheet
27/894525
A short, easy walk over
farmland to the castle.

Rait Castle lies two miles south of Nairn in a rural setting of rolling fields and tree-covered hills. The most direct route to the castle from Nairn is via the A939 (Grantown-on-Spey road). Two miles out of Nairn, you turn right on to the B9109 (Cawdor) road. After three-quarters of a mile you will come to a minor road marked 'Raitcastle Farm'. You can leave your car here and walk to the castle ruins, just over half a mile from the road.

Your walk takes you first along a tree-lined, metalled road, with a little burn on the right-hand side. At the farm buildings, the paving runs out and the way becomes rutted and bumpy and muddy in wet weather – a typical farm road, in fact. The remainder of the walk to the castle ruins is along the edge of a cultivated field.

The ruins of the castle stand in a thicket of thorn and brush and are sufficiently large to give you a good idea of what the castle must have looked like in the time of Lord Rait. There is a round tower, gothic-style window arches on two levels, and one door remaining of what was clearly quite a small castle.

THE SOUTH-WEST

23. THE WITCH OF AYR
Ayr

Witch hunts and trials became a regular and horrific event in Scottish society in the seventeenth century, and something like a thousand people were executed for witchcraft, with many more being imprisoned, banished, or otherwise punished for the crime.

The town of Ayr had its share of these trials, with the records showing six occasions on which witches were burned in the market place. The name Maggie Osborne does not appear in any of these records, which is surprising because the 'true details' of her life and activities are among the best-known of all Scottish witch stories, and the traditional tales about her can be dated back at least to the late seventeenth century.

One tradition has it that she was just an unfortunate girl named Margaret Osborne who developed a brain tumour which caused seizures so dreadful to behold that people thought she must be possessed by the Devil. She was pricked for the Devil's mark, was found to have one, was tortured, tried and finally burned.

Much more richly embroidered with detail is the tradition that puts Maggie Osborne firmly in the category of the witch as a wizened old woman complete with 'familiar' and cauldron for casting spells.

This Maggie Osborne was born into the witchcraft business, being the daughter of a famous warlock, the Laird of Fail. Almost as soon as Maggie could walk and talk, her father began instructing her in the magic arts until, still a young maiden, Maggie knew as much as and probably more than her father.

149

Reaching adulthood, Maggie Osborne chose to move to Ayr where she set up business as an innkeeper. She ran her inn well, providing clean beds and clear ale for the citizens of Ayr and visitors to the town for fifty years. But once the inn doors had been bolted for the night, Maggie Osborne's activities became very dubious – or so local people whispered to each other.

She would make frequent night journeys over the hills to Galloway, working her devilish spells on young women, housewives and farm animals. She always followed the same route over the Carrick Hills on these journeys, sitting nonchalantly on her broomstick as she flew over the rooftops and hedges. People could trace the course of 'Maggie's gate to Galloway' in the dry patches left in the grass on the hills by the feet of the imps from Hell who were her familiars on these trips. The sulphurous heat

The Carrick Hills.

from their feet dried out the earth and left it sterile, so that nothing ever grew on the spots again.

Two particularly unpleasant deeds were laid at Maggie's door. The first concerned a family against whom she had held a grudge ever since the night the husband, walking home over the Carrick Hills, had trodden on Maggie as she crawled along in the form of a shiny black beetle – something which the folks of Ayr swore she did quite frequently. This brush with death remained in Maggie's mind until she was able to exorcize it by killing the entire family; she buried them under a snowslide in the winter.

The second deed which weighed in the scales against Maggie Osborne was the raising of a fierce storm in the Bay of Ayr, during which a ship, against whose master she had had a grudge because of some imagined slight at her inn, was smashed on the St Nicholas rocks near Ayr harbour and foundered with all hands.

This last deed was Maggie's undoing, for a servant girl had seen her raising the storm in a bucket in her kitchen and had informed the town council.

Maggie Osborne was tortured, tried and found guilty of the crimes which were always set against witches:

> Ye, having shaken off all fears of god and rever-
> ence and regard of the divyne ordinance, Lawes
> and act of parliament of this kingdom has betaken
> yourself to the Service of Satan. And taken his
> mark upon your bodie, practised used and exer-
> cised divers and sundrie develish charmes,
> withchcraft and sorcerie . . .

Maggie remained remarkably composed when this terrible indictment was read out. She even smiled and cackled to herself as she sat in the courtroom. She certainly did not seem upset at the thought of being burned to death, as everyone in court agreed afterwards.

This, they all realized with hindsight, was undoubtedly because she had made a pact with the Devil and he had shown her how she might escape the fire in a way which would set Ayr by the ears for years afterwards.

As part of the Devil's plan, Maggie Osborne asked the judge if he would grant her one last request in this life. That, said the judge, depended on what it was. Maggie said that she wanted to carry into the fire with her two new pewter plates that had never been washed or touched by water in any way. It seemed a simple enough request, so the judge granted it.

A lad was sent off to get the pewter plates while Maggie was led out to the Fish Cross in the centre of the 'auld toon' of Ayr, where the crowds were waiting to see her die. Soldiers held them back and more soldiers surrounded the pile of faggots for the bonfire which was to be the old witch's funeral pyre.

The lad rushed forward, rather breathlessly, with the plates and handed them to Maggie Osborne. 'Are they new and never touched by water?' she asked him.

'Oh, yes,' he replied, thinking that what the old woman did not know she would not grieve over, so why tell her that on his way out of the kitchen he had slipped on a patch of water that had dripped on to the floor and dropped one of the plates; it had landed in the water, but he had dried it very carefully, so why tell Maggie of the incident?

Maggie attached the pewter plates to her shoulders and stepped on to the prepared bonfire. A soldier thrust a burning torch into the middle, and soon it was blazing fiercely, with the flames leaping high into the air. Suddenly, Maggie Osborne flapped her pewter 'wings' and rose up into the air, out of the reach of the flames and high above the heads of the astonished watchers. Just as it seemed that she would disappear altogether, one of her pewter 'wings' – the one the lad had dropped – fell off, and Maggie

Osborne plummeted back down to earth.

Her fall was broken when her petticoats caught round a projecting cornice, and there she hung, screaming imprecations at the Devil who had betrayed her when she had served him so long and so faithfully. A soldier reached up with his halberd, unhooked her, and thrust her back into the fire.

Thus died the Witch of Ayr.

THE WALK:	MAP SQUARE:
AN EASY HILL WALK – AS	Ordnance Survey Sheet
FAR AS YOU LIKE – ON	70/293169
THE CARRICK HILLS.	A ½ mile to 4½ mile walk.

The Fish Cross, where Maggie Osborne was burned, no longer exists; a cross of stones in the roadway marks where it stood opposite the south end of the Auld Brig. The Carrick Hills do still exist, of course. They lie south-west of Ayr, and are low, grass-covered and rolling. A walk across them, following the trail of Maggie Osborne, combines very well with a visit to the Robbie Burns sites in Alloway, so we suggest that, having looked at the Auld Brig and the site of the Fish Cross in Ayr, you drive out of town on the B7024 (signposted 'Burns Heritage Trail' in the centre of town) to Alloway.

Having visited the village – where you will find Burns' Cottage, Alloway Kirk, Brig o' Doon, the Grecian-style Burns Monument, as well as the very good Land o' Burns Visitor Centre – leave Alloway by the road to Doonfoot, turning left along the A719 (the coast road to Girvan) at the Doonfoot roundabout.

About three miles along the A719, you will come to a narrow turning on the left, signposted 'Carrick Hills'.

Follow this road past the farm buildings for just under a mile until you come to a farm gate where you may leave your car. Beyond the gate, the metalled, unfenced road meanders south-east over the rolling hill country, where cows and sheep graze oblivious of the presence of vehicles or people.

Brown Carrick Hill rises to the south and about half a mile from the farm gate a track goes off to the left towards the summit (904 feet). From here you can see out across Ayr Bay to the Firth of Clyde and inland to the farming country between Ayr and Maybole.

If you follow the road right across the hills for about four miles you will reach the B7024, with Maybole lying to the south and Alloway to the north.

24. THE ROASTING OF THE COMMENDATOR
Dunure Castle, near Ayr

The cliff-top, wind-swept site of the ruins of Dunure Castle lies on the Carrick coast, seven and a half miles south of Ayr. The fortress was once a stronghold of the Kennedys of Cassillis, who held extensive lands in western Ayrshire, though their principal seat was Culzean Castle, four and a half miles further south.

Dunure Castle on the Carrick Coast.

There is not much left of Dunure Castle today, though a fifteenth-century dovecot to one side indicates that it was once a dwelling as well as a fortress. A plaque on the castle wall suggests an eventful past, though, for it tells us that Gilbert Kennedy, fourth Earl of Cassillis, entertained Mary Queen of Scots here for four days in August 1563 and that the same earl was involved in the notorious episode of the roasting of the Commendator of Crossraguel Abbey in Dunure Castle on 1 September 1570.

It is possible that the first event had a bearing on the second, for entertaining a monarch and her attendant court was always an expensive business for a subject, however rich he might be in lands and other forms of wealth. Be that as it may, in the late 1560s Earl Gilbert began to cast covetous eyes in the direction of the wealthy agricultural lands of Crossraguel Abbey.

This splendid Cluniac monastery lying two miles south-west of Maybole, was well-endowed and its revenues were considerable. Hence, it was a fine object for government patronage, and its Commendator (or lay abbot), a man appointed to the position by the Privy Council, was obviously in an advantageous position for he had the use of the Abbey's revenues.

At the time of our story, the Commendator of Crossraguel Abbey was one Alan Stewart. He had obtained the Commendatorship on the death of the last abbot, Quentin Kennedy, who had been Earl Gilbert's uncle. In fact, Earl Gilbert had hoped to secure the Commendatorship on his own behalf and his failure to do so increased his animosity towards Alan Stewart.

Eventually, the earl's animosity turned from thought to deed. He kidnapped the Commendator, immuring him in the dank and dark vault beneath Dunure Castle until such time as he should agree to sign a charter passing the lands of Crossraguel and their revenues to Kennedy of Cassillis.

Alan Stewart was made of stern stuff and refused, so Earl Gilbert turned to torture. In that deep vault where no one might hear a man's screams, he roasted the Commendator, first covering him in soap. Although the flesh was burned from his legs and hands, the Commendator still refused to sign. Indeed, with his hands in such a ghastly condition he could hardly be expected to do so.

His object unachieved, Earl Gilbert departed from Dunure leaving the Commendator still imprisoned in the vault. His desperate plight was not unknown, however. Someone, perhaps one of the Earl's own people at Dunure, took word of it to Stewart's brother-in-law, Kennedy, Laird of Bargany, who had no love for the other Kennedy. The Laird of Bargany instantly despatched a party of his own men to rescue Alan Stewart, and they succeeded in forcing a way into Dunure Castle and throwing out Earl Gilbert's guard. Alan Stewart's plight was too desperate for him to be removed, so Stewart of Bargany's men lowered the portcullis and prepared to defend Dunure against its owner and any forces he might bring against them.

In the meantime, Stewart of Bargany had been raising forces of his own and soon descended on Dunure to relieve his garrison and rescue Stewart. The Commendator had recovered sufficiently from his ordeal to be able to denounce Earl Gilbert with some vigour from the Market Cross in Ayr. He also wrote to the Privy Council complaining of his wrongs, but he received little satisfaction. The Privy Council did summon Earl Gilbert to its presence to explain his deed but took little action, despite Kennedy of Bargany's fulminations. Earl Gilbert is believed to have paid the Commendator an annual sum in compensation, but that was all. In fact, a year later Earl Gilbert was able to gain possession of the Crossraguel Abbey properties simply by buying them.

For the rest of his life, Earl Gilbert appeared to suffer no remorse for his evil deed, which left a black stain on the history of the Kennedys of Cassillis. True, some people gave a wide berth to a man who was said to keep a black raven as his familiar in the vault of Dunure Castle, and others said that the Devil had surely marked the earl out for his own.

The latter viewpoint seemed vindicated when the earl died after being thrown from his horse five years later. A crow flew out of the sky and alighted on his coffin as it was being taken to Maybole for burial, and the horses were unable to pull the carriage along. As soon as the crow, which onlookers said must be the Devil's messenger in search of Earl Gilbert's soul, flew off, the horses were able to move forward again.

It is possible that the Devil already had the Earl of Cassillis's soul, for another story about his death tells how the Devil came to claim it the night the earl died.

The master of a ship sailing down the Firth of Clyde was startled to see coming out of the sunset towards his vessel what looked like a great ball of fire. As it drew closer, he saw that it was a fiery chariot and horses driven by a ghostly figure.

'Whence, and whither bound?' he cried.

'From Hell to Cassillis for the soul of the Earl!' came the reply from the chariot's driver.

And when, not long after, the fiery chariot flew back whence it had come, the howls and cries of its new passenger could plainly be heard above the sound of the sea and the wind.

THE WALKS:
1. FROM DUNURE CASTLE ALONG THE COURSE OF THE DISUSED RAILWAY LINE TO ELECTRIC BRAE.

MAP SQUARE:
Ordnance Survey Sheets:
1. 70/253158

2. A WHERE-YOU-WISH WALK IN CULZEAN COUNTRY PARK.

Two former homes of the Kennedys of Cassillis are the starting points of the easy walks here.

Dunure Castle is an easy drive from Ayr on the A719, which follows the coast down to Turnberry and Girvan. Culzean Castle also lies off this road, and from it you can circle over to Kirkoswald on the A77(T) where Robbie Burns' friend, Souter Johnnie, had his house (open afternoons, except Friday, from April to September), then on up the A77(T) to Crossraguel Abbey (open weekdays and Sunday afternoons) to Maybole, and so back to Ayr via Alloway with its rich associations with Robbie Burns – a very pleasant round trip.

The Ruins of Dunure Castle.

Our FIRST SUGGESTED WALK begins at Dunure Castle which lies on an unnumbered but well-signposted minor road off the A719. You can leave your car in the parking area on this road, and walk over the grass to see the castle close at hand.

From the castle, walk south down the minor road for just under half a mile until you come to the point where it runs by the course of the disused railway line. There is now a track down this line which, although it runs through several cuttings, also offers some good glimpses of sea and coast.

We suggest you walk down the line as far as Croy Brae (the Electric Brae), which is marked by a milestone between the road and the line. This is a distance of about a mile and a quarter, and allows you to investigate the strange phenomenon of the hill which apparently defies the law of gravity. They say it is an optical illusion and that what looks like the top of the hill is in fact about fifteen feet lower than the 'bottom'. We say that when we put our car in neutral and left the hand-brake off, it started moving backwards uphill. You will often find a car stopped on the Brae trying out the phenomenon.

For the *SECOND SUGGESTED WALK* in this area, drive down the A719 to Culzean Castle, once the chief seat of the Kennedys of Cassillis and now a National Trust for Scotland property, presented by the head of the Kennedy family, the Marquis of Ailsa, in 1945.

Surrounding the castle are the grounds of the Culzean Country Park, Scotland's first – opened in 1969. The park is always open, but the castle and the NTS Visitor Centre are open daily from April to October only.

The castle was designed by Robert Adam for the tenth Earl of Cassillis between 1777 and 1792 and is a truly magnificent building. Among its outstanding architectural features are an oval staircase and a round drawing room. The National Guest Flat in the castle was given to General (later President) Eisenhower for his lifetime use.

The Country Park, which covers 565 acres, and so gives you plenty of scope for walking, has several woodland walks and picnic spots. There are also a beautiful walled garden dating from 1783, a deer park, a swan pond, an aviary and a camellia house.

25. MICHAEL SCOT AND THE DEVIL
Glenluce

Glenluce lies in the south of Wigtownshire on the A75(T). It is a small town on the left side of the valley of the Water of Luce which runs along flat land before it empties into Glen Luce Bay over a sandy shore. On a minor road that runs up the valley of the Water of Luce is Glen Luce Abbey, site of one of the many legends woven round the famous twelfth-century Scottish astrologer and mathematician, Michael Scot. In legend, Michael Scot is a wizard and magician; in fact, he was one of the foremost scholars of his age.

The legend of Glen Luce Abbey tells how Michael Scot once kept the Plague a prisoner in the abbey's crypt, tied in a sack so that it could not harm anyone. This good deed pleased everybody except one. That person was the Devil, who had loosed the Plague on Scotland to create as much misery as possible. When the Devil heard that Michael Scot had had the effrontery not only to push the Plague unceremoniously into a sack but also to leave that sack in the crypt of Glen Luce Abbey he was most annoyed and immediately despatched his most unlovable demon to plague the life out of Michael Scot.

At first the demon, who was a lively and inventive chap, made a nuisance of himself in the manner of most demons, moving furniture around in the middle of the night, upsetting food that was cooking in pots and pans, setting fire to wood stores, frightening pigs and sheep, and so on. Then he tried more unpleasant tricks, such as taking the slates off the roof over Michael Scot's bed on a wet and windy night and making his mare go lame every time that

Michael Scot had to leave Glenluce to attend to business.

Finally, Michael Scot had had enough and he caught the demon by the tail and demanded to have a talk with him.

'All right,' the demon said. 'Just let go of my tail and tell me what you want.'

'I want to know,' Michael Scot said as the demon, having examined his tail to see if any damage had been done to it, now turned and faced him, 'I want to know what it takes to get rid of you.'

'Had you asked me sooner,' the demon replied, 'I would have told you sooner, but it would not have made any difference.'

'Well, tell me now,' Michael Scot said, 'and we will see.'

'Very well,' the demon said, 'to get rid of me you have to think of a task that I cannot do. Easy isn't it? Except, of course, that there is nothing I can't do with my supernatural power. I shall give you three chances.'

Michael Scot went away and thought about the most difficult thing that he knew about and remembered that though many had tried no one had yet succeeded in damming the River Tweed at Kelso. He told the demon about this and asked if he were able to do what everyone else had failed to do.

'Easy,' said the demon and disappeared in a puff of smoke.

Next morning the demon was waiting for Michael Scot at breakfast with a grin on his face. Michael Scot knew that the demon had bested him so he did not even bother to enquire how he had fared. Instead, he immediately set the demon another task. This time it was to go to the Eildon Hill at Melrose and split it into three.

Once again the demon set off with a mocking laugh, leaving a trail of smoke as he sped away over the hills. Even before he was back Michael Scot had decided that the task was too easy for such a cunning creature as his demon, so while his tormentor was away he examined his book of spells to see if it would suggest any way to get rid of the demon. Finding no inspiration there, Michael Scot went disconsolately for a walk along the Luce Sands which stretch for many a mile along the coast.

Suddenly, an idea came to him and the more he thought about it the better it seemed. Sure that he had now hit upon a task that even a demon could not manage he went home and made himself some tea.

The demon appeared just as Michael Scot was finishing his second bannock and he sat down and helped himself to a cup of tea in the irritatingly complacent manner of one who knows that he has scored over his opponent and is going to be condescending about it.

'To tell you the truth,' the demon said, 'the Eildon Hill job was not difficult. I am sure you can do better than that.'

'Oh, I don't know,' Michael Scot said. 'I'm getting rather disheartened.'

'Oh come on,' the demon replied. 'I'm sure you can think of something else.'

'Well,' said Michael Scot, 'as a matter of fact, I have thought of something. You know all that sand down at Luce Bay? Do you think it would be possible to make a rope of it?'

'Easy,' said the demon, whose earlier successes had gone to his head. 'Easy.'

'All right then,' said Michael Scot, 'that is your third task.'

The demon went off to the beach whistling a tune, promising to be back soon. Night fell, and there was no sign of him. Next day, Michael Scot ate his breakfast in peace. All day there was no sign of the demon, nor the next day, and after a week Michael Scot knew that the creature would not come back. In fact, the demon had found a job for eternity and if you walk on Luce Sands you can sometimes hear him cursing and muttering to himself as the tide sweeps across the beach, for he still has not discovered a way to make a rope out of sand.

<table>
<tr><td>THE WALK:
FROM KELSO TO
KALEMOUTH.</td><td>MAP SQUARE:
Ordnance Survey Sheet
74/725344
A 6-mile walk, along paths
and roads. The route is sign-
posted and is not difficult.</td></tr>
</table>

The tasks that Michael Scot set the demon were in three different locations. We have chosen the Kelso one for a walk, as the town and its surrounding countryside are full of places of interest, as well as being very pretty.

Kelso is on the River Tweed at the spot where it is joined by the Teviot, and ranks with Jedburgh in its charm and interest. The centre of the town, where the walk begins, is the great cobbled square dominated by a fine eighteenth-century court house.

The suggested walk is based on one devised by the local tourist office and the Planning and Development of the Borders Regional Council. Pamphlets including a map are usually available locally.

Start the walk by walking south-east out of the square along the main street, Bridge Street, which passes the Kelso Abbey. All that remains today of the once powerful abbey are the tower and transepts and ruins of bays, but it is still an imposing sight and worth stopping to look at. From the abbey, continue to the bridge (there is a good view of the town) and cross to the south bank, where you turn right along the A699.

After a few yards, you will reach the confluence of the Tweed and the Teviot, with the path taking you along the bank of the River Teviot. Cross this by Teviot Bridge, which brings you to its left bank. The path then takes you past a

Kelso Abbey.

cottage and over a stile and in less than half a mile you come to a large mound surmounted with a clump of trees and some fragments of old walls. This is all that remains of Roxburgh Castle, once one of the most powerful seats in the Border Country, around which spreads the old town of Roxburgh. The castle changed hands between Scots and English many times, and was in the hands of the English when the Scots took it in the fifteenth century, then the English utterly destroyed it in 1550. The town was reborn further up the river and is today a small village on our route.

Past the castle, your path follows the left (west) bank of the Teviot, which is pleasantly green and wooded, for two miles where it joins the road into Roxburgh village via a stile above Roxburgh Mill Farm. From the village, you take the signposted path under the railway bridge to the Teviot which you follow until you come to the track of the disused railway. You walk along this green and pleasantly overgrown cutting until you come to a road again which you climb down to via a stile and some steps. You then turn left and follow this road to Kalemouth where you take a bus back to Kelso. Alternatively, you can take the bus to Kalemouth or to Roxburgh from Kelso and walk back from either place. From Kelso to Roxburgh is just over three miles and to Kalemouth six miles.

A shorter walk from Kelso leaves the market square in a north-westerly direction. Turn left to reach the bank of the River Tweed and follow the path towards Floors Castle, which is just a mile away. The castle is the seat of the Duke of Roxburgh, and is open to the public from May to September.

Although first built in the eighteenth century, the castle was much altered in the nineteenth and therefore has a markedly Victorian aspect. It is set in pleasant parkland in which there is a monument marking the spot where James II of Scotland was killed by a cannon that burst during the Siege of Roxburgh by the Scots. —

167

26. THE SECRET OF HEATHER ALE
Mull of Galloway

The most southerly county in Scotland extends in a hammer-head shape from north to south off Wigtownshire, to which it is joined by an isthmus between Loch Ryan and Luce Bay. On the southernmost tip of this peninsula there is a promontory known as the Mull of Galloway. This cliff-girt headland is the most southerly point in Scotland, and its wild coastal scenery against which the Atlantic swell breaks ceaselessly, has much of the charisma of such other Scottish extremities as Cape Wrath and Duncansby Head at John O'Groat's.

The whole of Galloway has been inhabited since ancient times; at its centre at Stoneykirk, there remain three of the earliest Christian monuments in Britain and there are stones that tell of earlier, more legendary times. It is not surprising, then, to find at its southern extremity a tale of a secret recipe for an ambrosia fit for the gods. This was heather ale, an alcoholic beverage known only to the Picts, the recipe for which they guarded with their lives from the rapacious Scots who longed to know the secret of its manufacture.

At the end of the long wars between the Picts and Scots there remained only one man who knew the secret recipe. This was an ancient distiller of the wonder ale, who lived on the Mull of Galloway with his son.

Father and son lived on the cliffs above the restless sea and carried on their daily life as inconspicuously as possible, not telling a soul about their possession of the secret of the magic brew. One day, someone who had known the father from earlier and happier times when his brewing skill had been appreciated far and wide recognized the famous brewer and soon the word was passed around that the maker of heather ale was residing on the Mull of Galloway.

The gossip eventually came to the ears of a Scot who, while drinking in a local tavern, overheard one of the more indiscreet customers boasting about the quality of the heather ale made by the Pict of Galloway.

This news having been passed on to the Scottish invaders, it was not long before armed men were out in force looking for the brewer. Their orders were to extract the secret from the old man at whatever cost and then to do with him what they wanted.

One fine day, as the father and son sat making clay pots to hold their next supply of ale, a group of Scots arrived and, seizing them violently, demanded to be told the secret recipe. The father and the son feigned total ignorance of what they were asked for, but this only infuriated their captors. Seeing that intimidation was getting them nowhere, the Scots bound the old man and tied him to a rock. They then staked his son out on the ground.

Drawing their knives, they began to torture the young man, hoping that this would break the father's spirit and force him to reveal the secret of Pictish ale. Seeing his son in dreadful agony, the father found it difficult to resist the temptation to tell the Scots all they wanted to know.

'Will you promise to put him out of his agony if I tell you the secret?' he asked, in anguish.

'We will,' the leader of the Scots agreed.

'Very well,' the old man whispered, 'go ahead.'

He could not look as the Scots plunged their daggers into the young man's side. Waiting only to ensure that his son was indeed dead, he raised his head and laughed in the torturers' faces.

'Now you have no more hold on me,' he said defiantly.

'And you will never know the secret of heather ale.'

On hearing this, the leader of the Scots was seized with a terrible rage. He stepped towards the old man with his sword raised and slashed at him in a berserk fury. The ill-aimed blows, while grievously wounding his victim, also cut through his bonds, enabling him to stagger away from his assailant. He lunged towards the cliff and threw himself over the edge.

As the Scots watched the old man's body spiralling down to the foam-flecked rocks, they heard him laughing triumphantly. By his ruse, he had kept for eternity the secret which no one on earth would ever know; how to make the delectable brew called heather ale.

THE WALK:	MAP SQUARE:
FROM DRUMMORE TO THE LIGHTHOUSE AT THE MULL OF GALLOWAY.	Ordnance Survey Sheet 82/134365 A long cliff-top walk – 11 miles for the round trip – which can be considerably shortened by driving to the Tarbets.

The A75 from the English border at Gretna Green to Stranraer crosses southern Galloway via Dumfries and Gatehouse at Fleet. From Glasgow the A77 and A716 reach down to the Mull of Galloway. Stranraer is the embarkation point for ferries to Ireland and is therefore the terminus point for the railway from Glasgow and England. Apart from being a busy port, Stranraer is the main centre of tourist accommodation in Galloway. The main road from Stranraer down to the southern tip of the Mull, at Drummore, is the A77/A716.

Our WALK to the Mull of Galloway starts at Dunmore. This is a small village in the south of Galloway looking across

Luce Bay to Port William. From here you can walk south along the minor road past the castle to Maryport one and three-quarter miles away and then along the cliffs to Portankill (another one and three-quarter miles). On the way are the ruins of an old church and, as you climb along the cliff top, a building known as St Medan's Chapel, which is really a cave to which walls have been added.

At Portankill, you go inland and turn left at the road which goes south to the Tarbets at the isthmus between the mainland and the Mull of Galloway. From the few cottages of East and West Tarbet, it was about a mile to the Mull, with a track leading to the lighthouse and the 200-foot cliffs from which the last brewer of heather ale jumped to his death.

From the cliffs and the lighthouse (which the keeper may allow you to visit, if it is convenient), some splendid tidal patterns may be seen off the headland. On a clear day you are also supposed to be able to see seven ancient kingdoms from here: Scotland, England, Ireland, Wales, the Isle of Man, Kyle (now Ayrshire) – and Heaven! Behind you, a line of earthworks (clearly marked on the Ordnance Survey map), known as the 'Double Dykes', lies across the isthmus below the Tarbets; this is said to be the Picts' last defence against the Scots from the north.

If this whole walk, the cliff-top part of which is quite strenuous, sounds too arduous, you can drive as far as the Tarbets and then walk the mile to the lighthouse.

ISLAY AND KINTYRE

The Piper of Keil
The Sword of Islay

27. THE PIPER OF KEIL
Kintyre

On the southern coast of Kintyre, where the B842 passes through the village of Southend and peters out into a minor road, lies Keil Point. St Columba landed here on his first mission from Ireland. There is a ruined chapel near the road with a flat-topped rock nearby. St Columba is said to have built the chapel and to have stood on the rock to take a last look at Ireland, and indentations in the rock are supposed to be his footprints.

Behind the point the land rises to a hill called Cnoc Mor and to the west Glen Breackerie reaches the sea across a flat valley which rises steeply again into the hills that stretch to the Mull of Kintyre, the most westerly point of the peninsula.

This far-away area of Scotland, surrounded by sea at the end of the long Kintyre peninsula, is a popular place for those who like an unspoilt but not too rugged landscape, and to the east of Keil there are parks for caravans as well as a camping site which attract summer visitors.

The hamlet of High Keil is situated about half a mile from the point beneath which lie the caves where the Piper of Keil disappeared never to return.

According to the story, this piper – whose name was Alasdair – was the best piper in Kintyre, if not in the whole of Scotland. He was always much in demand for dances, weddings and other celebrations. This popularity and the constant adulation he received made the piper a little boastful, a fault which became more evident after he had taken a dram or two of whisky, as was his habit while he played.

One day Alasdair was asked to play at a celebration held near the Point of Keil and as the evening wore on and the drink flowed more and more freely, some of the dancers, their imaginations perhaps more unrestrained than usual, began to say that Alasdair's playing that night almost rivalled that of the faery people.

This was an exaggerated claim, of course, for the faery people, being supernatural, were capable of feats far beyond the range of ordinary mortals. Soon an argument developed, with some people siding with the dancers who claimed that Alasdair was equal to any faery musician that cared to show up, and others saying that it was impossible to equal the Little People. How either faction could hope to settle the point once and for all, no one bothered to say.

Among those present there were more than a few who were worried that the argument, which was being conducted in loud and even angry voices, must be well within earshot of the Little People, who were known to reside in the large cave in the cliff by Keil Point. They were afraid that the faeries would take offence and that they would show their displeasure by playing those unpleasant tricks that irritated faeries were wont to visit on ordinary people, like turning milk sour, or causing furniture to dance about for no reason, or even stealing children and leaving changelings in their place.

The anxiety of these more cautious participants of the celebrations was not unfounded, for the hullabaloo had indeed reached the ears of the faeries and even the queen herself, who stopped to listen carefully to what was going on outside her cave territory.

It was unfortunate that at this moment Alasdair himself decided to take part in the argument and boldly declared that he could pipe any faery into submission should one of them wish to appear and compete with him. This was the whisky talking, of course, but as far as the Queen of the

176

Faeries was concerned, it was an insult that could not be allowed to go unpunished. She set about weaving a spell which soon drew Alasdair inexorably towards the cave, still shouting as he went that he would show the faeries what good piping really was.

With Alasdair went his terrier which, like most dogs, was irrationally devoted to its master and, had it been able to speak, would undoubtedly have confirmed Alasdair's claim to be a better piper even than the faeries.

Seeing Alasdair disappearing into the black cave, everyone came abruptly to his senses, instantly stopping the debate. They all were suddenly seized with great apprehension. 'Come back,' they called. 'Come back.' But Alasdair, piping away as he walked boldly into the cave with his little dog at his heels, did not hear them. Or if he did, he chose to ignore them.

As the sound of Alasdair's pipes faded into the depths of the cave, the company fell silent, fearing for his safety. As time went by and he did not reappear their fears increased, though no one offered to go in to look for him. They waited and waited, afraid to search for him but also reluctant to go home. Then, suddenly, they heard the frightened yelping of Alasdair's dog which tore out of the cave with its hair on end and its eyes dilated as if it had seen the Devil himself. The terrier ran through the crowd and disappeared along the beach never to be seen again . . . Neither was Alasdair, though people say that at night the sound of his pipes can still be heard to this day issuing from the depths of the cave and playing a slow, sad lament.

THE WALK:	MAP SQUARE:
FROM CARSKIEY TO	Ordnance Survey Sheet
MULL LIGHTHOUSE	68/657079
AND BACK.	A strenuous walk, $9\frac{1}{2}$ miles for the round trip, across the Mull of Kintyre.

Keil Point can be reached by road from Campbeltown, on the A83/B842 via Southend, or by branching off on to the minor and steep road which comes down Glen Breackerie to reach Keil Point from the west. The land at the southern end of Kintyre is hilly and sparsely populated and the coast is rocky. There is plenty of open ground to walk on round Keil Point as well as tracks to follow with various points of interest. An interesting and strenuous walk is from the western side of Glen Breackerie to the Mull of Kintyre.

Leave the car at Carskiey over Strone Water. Ahead lies a road, nearly five miles long, which near its western end drops 1,200 feet in one and a half miles. The road is also steep as it climbs a valley to Torr Dubh (923 feet). Past here, it follows the side of a hill and crosses two streams before it reaches more level ground above Borgadel Water which flows down to the coast on your left. Climbing slowly, you now approach the head of the valley with Torr Mor (1,345 feet) on your left and Beinn na Lice (1,390 feet) on your right. You now walk through The Gap, between the two, and start descending steeply towards Mull Lighthouse, which was built in 1787 and which you may visit on weekdays in summer. There is a car park by the lighthouse. Views all round are very fine, with Ireland only thirteen miles to the west and the Mull of Kintyre (made world-famous by Paul McCartney's song of praise) to the south.

28. THE SWORD OF ISLAY
Islay, Hebrides

Islay, which lies to the west of Kintyre and is separated from Jura by the mere half mile of the Sound of Islay, is an attractive island popular with summer visitors who stay at the hotels and bed-and-breakfast places in the six main villages scattered over the 20- by 25-mile island.

Islay is a quiet unspoilt place with a plentiful bird life and lochs well stocked with trout and salmon.

Islay.

On Islay's south side is vast Laggan Bay whose beach stretches for several miles and which lies between the peninsula of the Rhinns of Islay and the strangely named Mull of Oa. To the east of Oa lies Port Ellen, the main commercial centre and port for the ferries that come from Tarbet.

In this idyllic place there once lived a smith named Alasdair Strongarm who was a skilled maker of swords. Alasdair was a widower and lived with his son. Now Islay was said to be the home of many of the Little Folk who may be found all over Scotland, but particularly in the western parts, and Alasdair knew that they had a habit of carrying away attractive children like his son to bring them up in their own way. Alasdair, therefore, took care always to pick a rowan branch and keep it over the door of his house at night, to ward off any Little Folk who might choose to come near.

On one occasion, when he had to go away on business, he carefully reminded his son to place the rowan branch over the door before going to bed, but the lad forgot. When Alasdair returned from his travels he was shocked to find that a distinct change had come over his boy during his absence.

Suspecting immediately that this had something to do with the faeries, Alasdair consulted a local wise man who told him that it was probable that the child in his home was not his son at all but an imposter placed there by the Little Folk who had kidnapped his own boy. The only way to find out for sure, the wise man said, would be to carry out some tests. First Alasdair was to surround his fireplace with empty eggshells filled with water, and then he must report back to the wise man what the boy said.

That night, Alasdair did as he was told, putting the eggshells carefully round the fire. As he was completing the task, he heard a strange cackle of laughter from the bed where the boy lay, and then he heard him mutter, 'Never in my eight hundred years have I seen the like of that.'

Alasdair hurried out of the house and recounted the episode to the wise man who nodded with satisfaction at having his theory proved right. Clearly only a supernatural being could claim to having lived eight hundred years. Now, the wise man told Alasdair, he must get the changeling out of the house and follow him to where his true son was being kept a prisoner by the faeries. To achieve this, Alasdair must light a fire and throw the changeling into it.

Though Alasdair was reluctant to burn the faery child – what if he were his own son, after all – he nevertheless was prepared to do so if that was the way to get his son back. He went back home and lit the fire and before the faery could escape, Alasdair had grasped him by one of his skinny legs, which he now saw was that of an ancient man, and threw him on the flames. With a scream of rage and pain, the faery – now transformed into a wizened old man – shot out of the house, with Alasdair – pausing only to gather up a rowan branch and the Holy Bible he kept by his bed – in hot pursuit.

Following the howling faery up hill and down dale until he thought his lungs would burst, Alasdair suddenly saw him disappear into a large cave from which came the sound of singing and shouting. Now, usually any human who gets caught up in a faery dance goes on and on dancing and is not released until he has become on old man, but Alasdair was protected by his rowan branch, his Bible and his determination to get his son back. Pushing his way through the throng he went further and further into the cave until he came to the great glowing forges where the faeries made their magic swords and there he saw his son hard at work. Taking him by the arm, he ran back to the entrance of the cave, scattering the Little Folk before him and finally bursting out into the fresh air with the curses of the Faery

181

Queen ringing in his ears.

'Your son will never speak again,' she screamed. 'Never until he can break the spell that binds him.'

When they finally reached home and safety, Alasdair realized that what the faery had said was true; his son could no longer speak. To make up for his misfortune, Alasdair cared for his son more than he had ever done before, protecting him from the ordinary blows of daily life and giving him only the easiest jobs to do in the forge and at home.

One day, while he was making a sword, Alasdair was called outside by the wise man whose counsel had helped him get his son back. While he was gone, his son picked up the red-hot metal Alasdair had been hammering on the anvil and continued to work it in the way that he had been taught by the faeries. When his father returned he refused to give up his almost finished sword and pushed him aside. Alasdair looked at the expert way in which his son was working and seeing the look of total concentration on his face, decided to let him have his way. An hour went by and then another as the sword was heated and cooled and hammered and finally sharpened to a razor's edge. When it was finished, Alasdair knew that there had never been such a sword made in Islay by human hands, and that his son's skill had been learnt from the Little Folk. As he was meditating in this way and thinking that now not he but his son was the best sword maker in Islay, his son suddenly spoke.

Alasdair, by contrast, was silent in amazement, but soon realizing that the spell had been broken, he embraced the boy and the two danced round the room for joy.

Neither knew exactly what had happened to break the faeries' curse, but as Alasdair examined the sword he realized that only faery magic could have made it. He was sure that the forging of the sword had itself been the act that had broken the spell and that only his own over-protection of his son had prevented the boy's earlier liberation.

THE WALK: MAP SQUARE:
FROM UPPER KILLEYAN   Ordnance Survey Sheet
TO MULL OF OA.   60/365453
                             A 1½-mile walk each way
                             along tracks and rough paths.

Islay is the most southerly of the islands of the Hebrides, and may be reached by car ferry from Kennacraig, Kintyre (calling either at Port Ellen or Port Askaig) and by air from Glasgow (a summer service to Islay Aerodrome on Laggan Bay). A postal mini-bus service makes regular weekday runs between Port Askaig, Bridgend Bowmore, the airport and Port Ellen.

The area of Islay in which we have suggested a walk, the Oa, is not served by public transport, so we are assuming that you have brought your car to Islay or have hired one in Port Ellen; the walk from Port Ellen to Oa is approximately five miles, making the round trip rather long.

To reach the start of our suggested walk to the Mull of Oa, drive west out of Port of Ellen round Port Imeraval and the top of Kilnaughton Bay, following the Oa road which runs down across the centre of the peninsula for about four miles. Much of this land is virtually uninhabited, with great tracts owned by a millionaire who uses it as a sporting estate.

At the point where the metalled road ends, and unpaved tracks go off north-west to Lower Killeyan and south-west to Upper Killeyan, leave your car and follow the latter track for about three-quarters of a mile to Upper Killeyan Cottage where the track runs out. A rough path leads you gently uphill for another three-quarters of a mile to the Mull of Oa, where the viewpoint (424 feet above sea level) is splendid. The monument here was erected by the American Red Cross in memory of the men of two United States troopships which were lost here. The Tuscania *was torpedoed off the Oa in 1918 and the* Otranto *was driven on to the Rhinns of Islay after a collision in the same year. The scenery all around is splendidly wild and bleak, and the coast is a mass of cliffs and caves. It is no wonder the whole lonely peninsula was once used by smugglers and distillers of illicit whisky.*

SCOTTISH WALKS AND LEGENDS
WESTERN SCOTLAND AND THE HIGHLANDS
by Janice Anderson and Edmund Swinglehurst

The Ghost of Duntulum Castle
The Massacre at Glencoe
St Columba and the Loch Ness Monster
The Five Sisters of Kintail

This book is for the visitor to the Highlands and Western
Scotland (including the Islands) who wants to see the best of
their varied scenery and at the same time learn something of the
region's rich heritage. Janice Anderson and Edmund
Swinglehurst have selected the most fascinating legends of the
area and in each case give full details of how to reach their
location and the best way to explore the area on foot. Most of
the walks are short and easy, suitable for taking children along
– a few are longer to suit the more energetic.

ILLUSTRATED

£1.50

ALSO AVAILABLE IN THE WALKS AND LEGENDS
SERIES PUBLISHED BY GRANADA PAPERBACKS

LAKELAND WALKS AND LEGENDS
by Brian J Bailey   £1.50

LONDON WALKS AND LEGENDS
by Mary Cathcart Borer   £1.25

WEST COUNTRY WALKS AND LEGENDS
by J H N Mason   £1.25

WELSH WALKS AND LEGENDS
by Showell Styles   £1.00

SCOTTISH WALKS AND LEGENDS VOLUME 1
by Janice Anderson and Edmund Swinglehurst   £1.50

*All these books are available at your local bookshop or newsagent, or can be
ordered direct from the publisher. Just tick the titles you want and fill in the
form below.*

Name ....

Address ....

....

Write to Granada Cash Sales, PO Box 11, Falmouth, Cornwall TR10 9EN

Please enclose remittance to the value of the cover price plus:

UK: 40p for the first book, 18p for the second book plus 13p per copy for
each additional book ordered to a maximum charge of £1.49.

BFPO and EIRE: 40p for the first book, 18p for the second book plus 13p
per copy for the next 7 books, thereafter 7p per book.

OVERSEAS: 60p for the first book and 18p for each additional book.

*Granada Publishing reserve the right to show new retail prices on covers, which
may differ from those previously advertised in the text or elsewhere.*